Cooking With Elvis

When an amateur Elvis impersonator is paralysed in a car crash, his wife and daughter are forced to cope with the aftermath. Jill tries to replace him with cooking, Mam tries to replace him with sex. Unfortunately, they both try out their talents on the same man.

Part knockabout farce, part cookery course, part philosophical investigation, *Cooking With Elvis* is a provocative and outrageously funny look at disability while enjoying the three greatest pleasures in the world – sex, food and the King.

Bollocks

Inspired by Ernst Toller's neglected masterpiece *Hinkemann*, *Bollocks* is an examination of the impotence of lives ruined by war. Looking at an emasculated society where small lives are dominated by big business ideology, this intense yet darkly humorous work is about the emotional scars that follow physical pain.

Lee Hall's theatre work includes translations of Buchner's *Leonce and Lena* (Gate Theatre), Brecht's *Mr Puntilla and his Man Matti* (The Right Size/Almeida, Traverse and West End), *Mother Courage and her Children* (Shared Experience) and *A Servant to Two Masters* (RSC and Young Vic). His adaptation of his award-winning radio play *Spoonface Steinberg* premiered at the Crucible Theatre, Sheffield, in December 1999 and opened at the New Ambassadors Theatre, London, in January 2000. Originally broadcast on Radio 4 in 1995 as *Blood Sugar*, *Cooking With Elvis* (Live Theatre, Newcastle, and Edinburgh Festival 1999) opened in the West End in February 2000. Lee is currently filming *Dancer*, directed by Stephen Daldry, and will shortly be filming an adaptation of his prize-winning radio play *I Love You Jimmy Spud*. His television work includes *Ted and Alice*, *The Student Prince* and *Spoonface Steinberg*.

by the same author

A Servant to Two Masters
Spoonface Steinberg

Lee Hall

Cooking With Elvis
&
Bollocks

Methuen Drama

Published by Methuen Drama

First published in Great Britain by
Methuen Publishing Ltd

ISBN 0 413 74860 X

A CIP catalogue record for this book is available at the British Library

Typeset by SX Composing DTP, Rayleigh, Essex
Transferred to digital printing 2004

Caution

Cooking With Elvis

Cooking With Elvis was originally performed as the Radio 4 play *Blood Sugar* on 11 January 1995. The cast was as follows:

Grandma	Elizabeth Kelly
Mam	Charlie Hardwick
Jill	Sharon Percy
Billy	Trevor Fox

Director Kate Rowland

The stage play *Cooking With Elvis* was first performed at Live Theatre, Newcastle-upon-Tyne, on 14 October 1998. The same production opened at the Assembly Rooms, Edinburgh, on 6 August 1999. The cast was as follows.

Dad	Joe Caffrey
Stuart	Trevor Fox
Mam	Charlie Hardwick
Jill	Sharon Percy

Director Max Roberts
Designer Liz Cooke

Scene One

*Theatre in darkness. 'Thus Spake Zarathustra' by Strauss gets louder and louder. A match lights a gas hob which lights **Jill**'s face.*

Jill   Scene One. The Prologue. I was standing there with a spatula when they said you were dead.

*Lights up. **Jill** is standing with a wok. She adds oil.*

There was some linguine and a jar full of capers and some nice marinaded olives and they were going on about tubes and intensive care and what a terrible shame it was et cetera. And then they brought in Mam and we went downstairs and all her mascara had run and she was moaning on and everything and I said she better hurry up or the pasta would be boiled to a glue. And then she started shaking and that, and I was in my apron, and then she told me, that in fact there'd been a miracle, and in fact you weren't dead and somehow you'd pulled through. And thought sod the linguine and started to cry.

She has been cooking furiously throughout the speech. She adds more ingredients. And towards the end of the speech she flambés the contents of the wok.

And there at that point something changed deep inside me. Something changed that was good. You see, in my whole life up until that point, in my whole life, I was the one who was always left out, I was the one stuck in my bedroom, I was the one nobody fancied, I was the one they always called fatty, I was the one with the hideous hairband, I was the one who couldn't stop burping, always in her shadow, always the one without a clue. But suddenly, in that special moment, everything became clear and I saw a reason, a purpose, a mission, like a beacon in the darkness, a guiding star in the night, and I just looked at them through the pain and the tears and the anguish and I said: 'Take me back to domestic science.'

She pours the contents of the wok into a pie crust, pops on the top and puts it in the oven.

And they did.

Sampled intro to 'Jailhouse Rock'. Lights snap out. A hand reaches into the room from the doorway and switches on the light. It is the living room and the lighting this time is 'late-night seduction' from a standard lamp. **Mam** *comes in dressed to kill (maybe herself) and* **Stuart** *comes in, in specs. He seems nervously out of his depth.*

Scene Two

Jill   Scene Two. The Living Room.

Stuart   Mind, you've got a lovely house.

Mam   Shh.

Stuart   What's that smell?

Mam   Watch where you're walking.

Stuart   Bloody hell. What's that?

Stuart *sees the tortoise and picks it up.*

Mam   That's Stanley. Do you fancy a drink?

Stuart   Cush.

Mam   I've got a dry white in the fridge.

Stuart   I beg your pardon?

Mam   Dry white.

Stuart   Haven't you got beer.

Mam   I might have some lager.

Stuart   I divvint like wine, me. Here, I thought these were banned.

Mam   It's only a tortoise.

Stuart   I know. I thought there was a crisis on *Blue Peter*. Cheers. How much did you pay for this?

Mam   I don't know. I got it from Safeway's.

Stuart   My brother-in-law goes down to Dieppe, you know. He could save you thirty pee a can.

Mam   Stuart. Why don't you put the tortoise down.

Stuart   Pernod. Metaxax. The whack.

Mam   You seem very interested in food and drink, Stuart.

Stuart   What do you mean, like?

Mam   Well, ever since we got in the taxi, it's all you've talked about.

Stuart   Sorry. I tend to go on a bit. Especially about tarts. It's a professional interest. Cakes and stuff.

Mam   You're a baker?

Stuart   Not exactly. I'm a supervisor.

Mam   Of bakers.

Stuart   Of cakes. We make a load of stuff for Marks and Sparks.

Mam   Really.

Stuart   You know them Christmas puddings? We start making them in July. June sometimes.

Mam   Don't they go off?

Stuart   No. They're Christmas puddings. Aren't they?

Mam   Why did you come here, Stuart?

Stuart   Here?

Mam   No. Tynemouth Priory.

Stuart   I divvint knaa. For a drink and that.

Mam   For a drink?

Stuart   Well, you know.

Mam   Do you think I'm attractive, Stuart?

Stuart   Well, you're very nice-looking. I suppose.

Mam   How old do you think I am, Stuart?

Stuart   I don't know. I'm terrible at ages, me.

Mam   Have a guess.

Stuart   I don't know. You seem very mature.

Mam   Mature!

Stuart   Sophisticated, I mean. Wey most lasses don't know their arse from their elbow. Where as you seem, you know, very knowledgeable.

Mam   Would you like another drink, Stuart?

Stuart   I'm OK with this one. I try and keep an interest in things myself, like. You know, expand me horizons.

Mam   What sort of horizons, Stuart?

Stuart   I don't know. Like them programmes about frogs and stuff.

Mam   Have you ever tried tantric sex?

Stuart   I beg your pardon?

Mam   It's like sexual yoga. You bond together and make love without moving. Sting does it for ten hours at a time.

Stuart   You'd be lucky to get ten minutes out of me.

Mam   I don't know.

Stuart   I get winded running for the bus. It was a joke.

Mam   Stuart. Do you think I'm attractive?

Stuart   Yes.

Mam   You know you have a lovely physique, Stuart.

Stuart Have I?

Mam You have the body of an athlete. Do you train?

Stuart I like to have a knock around every so often.

Mam You know, Stuart, you really turn me on.

Stuart Thanks very much.

Stuart *stares at* **Mam**. *Knocks back his drink and lunges to kiss her.*

Mam What you doing?

Stuart I don't know. I thought I'd give you a kiss.

Mam Stand over there.

Stuart Eh?

Mam I want to look at you.

Stuart Go on then.

Mam Take your shirt off, Stuart.

Stuart What?

Mam Take it off. Now.

Stuart Like this?

Mam Over there. I want to see all of you, Stuart.

Stuart I feel embarrassed.

Mam Believe me, Stuart. You have nothing to be embarrassed about. The trousers.

Stuart Are you sure about this?

Mam For Christ's sake just shut up for five minutes, Stuart. I want you to touch yourself.

Stuart What do you mean?

Mam I want you to caress yourself, Stuart.

Stuart What do you mean, like? Have a wank?

Mam   For God's sake, just take off your Y-fronts, will you.

Stuart   All right. Calm down.

Stuart *hesitates.*

Mam   Now!

Stuart *gets them halfway down, baring his arse to the audience, when there is a banging at the door.* **Jill** *comes in.*

Stuart   Fucking hell.

Jill   Mam, he's doing it again.

Mam   Go away, darling.

Jill   Mam. He's having a fit.

Stuart   Who the hell are you?

Jill   I'm the daughter.

Stuart   But you must be fifteen!

Jill *wheels in* **Dad**. *He is having a fit.*

Mam   Jesus Christ, Jill. Can't you sort him out for yourself?

Jill   Mam. He's your husband.

Stuart   Frigging hell.

Mam   Watch your language. Did you give him his medicine?

Jill   Of course I gave him his medicine.

Stuart   What's the matter with him?

Jill   What's it look like. He's paralysed, you stupid idiot.

Stuart   Hey, don't call me a stupid idiot.

Mam   Shut it, you.

Jill   He gets these fits sometimes, there's nothing we can do about it.

Stuart   Maybe we should call an ambulance.

Jill   Look, just help to get him sitting up.

Mam *is pouring herself another drink.*

Jill   Mam. What are you doing?

Mam   Getting another drink. What does it look like?

Jill   Put that down at once. Please help me, Mam. Look at him.

Stuart   Look. Here.

Stuart *tries to move* **Dad** *but as he does so* **Dad** *pisses on* **Stuart** *and* **Dad** *falls to the floor.*

Jill   What are you doing?

Stuart   He's pissed himself.

Jill   You've dropped him.

Stuart   Oh no.

Jill   Oh Christ, man. It's all right, Dad.

Stuart   Look, it's all over iz.

Jill   Well, it's a good job you're not wearing any clothes then.

Mam   This is bloody typical. You haven't got any consideration, have you?

Jill   It's not my fault he's having a fit.

Stuart *struggles with* **Dad**.

Stuart   How long has he been like this?

Jill   Two years. He had an accident.

Stuart   You never said anything to me about a crippled husband.

Mam   You never asked, sweetheart.

Jill   He can't speak or anything. We think he's a bit depressed.

Stuart   I'm not surprised.

Mam   He's not depressed, Jilly. It's that bloody medication.

Stuart   I think he's nodding off now.

Mam   You just did this to embarrass me. Didn't you?

Jill   Of course I didn't.

Mam   You're perverse. You know that.

Jill   Mam. I am not perverse.

Mam   Just because you're jealous.

Jill   Jealous. Of him.

Stuart   What's wrong with me, like?

Mam   Nobody's asking your opinion. It's pathological this, Jill. Every bloody time I try and enjoy myself. You're a fucking embarrassment.

Stuart   Look, it's not embarrassing. Not really.

Mam   Of course it's embarrassing.

Stuart   No, honest. This sort of thing probably happens every day.

Mam   Don't be ridiculous.

Jill   I think you should put some pants on.

Stuart   There's nothing to be ashamed about.

Mam   Who said I'm ashamed? You're the one standing about covered in piss.

Jill   Mam, he's trying to be nice.

Stuart   It's all right. I think she's just had too much to drink.

Mam   You cheeky bastard.

Stuart   I was only saying.

Jill   I think you'd better go.

Stuart   Well, it's very nice to meet you both.

Mam   Get out will you. And mind that bloody tortoise.

Stuart *picks up his clothes and leaves sheepishly.* **Jill** *stares at* **Mam** *who is pouring another glass.*

Mam   What are you looking at?

Blackout.

Scene Three

Jill   Scene Three. Breakfast. I am not fat.

Mam   I'm not saying you're fat. All I said was you should watch those chocolate puddings.

Jill   Shut up, will you. There's nothing wrong with chocolate puddings.

Mam   You'll end up looking like a chocolate pudding if you're not careful. I've got nothing against chocolate puddings per se. It's just not right eating them for breakfast. Have you any idea what's in a chocolate pudding?

Jill   Three hundred and fifty calories.

Mam   Three hundred and fifty-eight calories, darling.

Jill   What were you doing last night?

Mam   It's your funeral. And don't change the subject.

Jill   Who was that man?

Mam   That was not a man, darling. That was Stuart.

Jill   Jesus Christ.

Mam   Don't Jesus Christ me, young lady. Didn't you like him?

Jill   Well, he wasn't exactly Mr Intellectual.

Mam   He was quite good-looking.

Jill   Mam, he was a complete divvy.

Mam   You don't understand anything, do you. I thought he was quite sensitive considering.

Jill   Considering you made him strip off and Dad pissed all over him.

Mam   Don't start blaming me for your father's bodily functions.

Jill   Mam. I don't see why you have to keep bringing them back.

Mam   Where else am I going to go? I've got you and your dad to think of.

Jill   Mam, can't you do an evening class or something?

Mam   Listen, Jill. I am thirty-eight years of age and my life isn't going to stop just because your dad's a vegetable.

Jill   Mam. Dad is not a vegetable. He says things.

Mam   Jill. He does not say things.

Jill   He understands. He understands everything.

Mam   Jill. You have got to stop denying the facts, darling. Dad is a cabbage and that's that. End of story.

Jill   But Mam, what'll people think?

Mam   What do you mean, what will people think?

Jill   The other week someone at school saw you getting off with Helen Storey's brother.

Mam   What were they doing down the Bigg Market?

Jill   Mam, he only just went to university.

Mam Jill. He told me he was twenty-seven.

Jill Mam. It's just not natural.

Mam What's natural. Sitting in your bedroom stuffing barrel-loads of custard creams down your neck till you blow up like a balloon.

Jill Mam. I am not a balloon.

Mam You want to look at yourself in the mirror, young lady.

Jill Mam. You're not supposed to behave like this. You're an English teacher.

Mam What's that got to do with anything?

Jill It's ridiculous. Going round like one of Pan's People.

Mam I do not look like one of Pan's People. Anyway, just because I'm an English teacher does not mean I have to lock myself up like Mother Teresa.

Jill Mam. Mother Teresa is dead.

Mam It's been two years, Jill. What do you expect me to do. I'm in the prime of life, Jilly.

Jill You are not in the prime of life, Mam. Anyway, there's no need to be picking fellas up. There are other things you can do.

Mam I suppose you'd have me down the whist drive with Auntie Irene.

Jill Mam. There are other ways of achieving satisfaction you know.

Mam I don't know why I bother listening to you.

Jill Mam. You could masturbate.

Mam I don't believe I'm hearing this.

Jill It's perfectly natural.

Mam   Listen, if you think I'm going to sit round here wanking my fingers to the bone for your benefit you've got another thing coming.

Jill   It's not for my benefit. It was just a suggestion. So you wouldn't have to go round like a dog's dinner.

Mam   At least I try to look attractive.

Jill   Who are you trying to impress, like? The cake man?

Mam   You're jealous, aren't you. That's what's going on here.

Jill   Mam. I am not getting jealous. All I'm saying is you won't admit to the fact that you're getting old.

Mam   I am not getting old. I think I look rather glamorous.

Jill   You do look glamorous. You just don't look like a mam. Have you ever thought of him stuck in his chair?

Mam   All I ever do is think about him stuck in his bloody chair.

Jill   Mam. That man was virtually naked.

Mam   The trouble is I treat you too much like an adult and you have no real understanding.

Jill   Mam, I do understand.

Mam   No you don't, lover. How could you. Look, just leave me alone to my life and I'll leave you alone to your cooking.

Jill   Does that mean I can have the birthday party?

Mam   I don't think that's a good idea.

Jill   It might stimulate him.

Mam   It won't stimulate him.

Jill   It might jolt his memory.

Mam   Please, darling.

Jill   Just because he's a vegetable doesn't mean he can't have a birthday party.

Mam   OK, please your Bessie. But for God's sake, no chocolate puddings.

Blackout.

Scene Four

Jill *lights a match and then the thirty-nine candles on the huge birthday cake, which lights her up. Dad is next to her but in darkness.*

Jill   Scene Four. Birthday Preparations. Sometimes I think about why we are here. If there's a purpose, to what it all means in the long-term. I mean it's weird, on the one hand, that some people are like beautiful and happy and all that, like Cherie Blair or that bloke off the telly. And then there are some people that are fat or crippled or just miserable like Mam. And I wonder why is it some people get all this misery and suffering and others are just happy all the time. But then probably Cherie Blair isn't all that happy underneath and the fella on the telly is probably on drugs or sleeps with children and that. So maybe nobody's happy – not fundamentally – not deep down. Maybe everybody has a longing – a longing things were different – a longing that people'd get better, longing that she'd shut up, or just longing for a nice piece of pie, or a rhubarb crumble, or a tandooried mackerel or something. Longing for something to fill you up. And maybe it'll be a torte, Dad, or a cabbage or a slice of quiche. It might be something continental or something from the Pacific rim; a steak-and-kidney pudding or just one of them things from Marks and Spencer's. But one day it'll wake you up, Dad. Like a resurrection, and you'll jump up, shake your hips again, and you'll kiss Mam and hold me, and we'll all be back together again.

There is a murmur from **Dad**. *'E . . . e . . . e . . .'*

Dad?

Another murmur. 'E . . . e . . . e.'

What was that, Dad. What were you trying to say?

Murmur. 'E . . .'

What was it, Dad? Elvis?

The lights go up fully and we see **Dad** *is dressed in his Elvis costume.* **Jill** *places a paper crown on his head from a cracker and blows a twizzle thing.*

Scene Five

Jill   Scene Five. The Party. Happy birthday. Come on, Mam.

Mam   Happy birthday. For God's sake take that hat of him.

Jill   It's his birthday.

Mam   It's macabre.

Jill   No it isn't.

Mam   For God's sake, Jilly.

Jill   For once in your life try to have a meal without complaining.

Mam   I just don't think it's very appropriate to dress him like this any more.

Jill   It's completely appropriate. It's like Elvis the King.

Mam   Jill, your dad is crippled.

Jill   But that's what he likes, Elvis Presley.

Mam   He doesn't like Elvis Presley. He doesn't like anything. What on earth is this, Jilly?

Jill   Chitterlings.

Mam   And what are chitterlings, darling?

Jill   Pigs' intestines.

Mam   For God's sake.

Jill   They're nice, Mam. It's what Elvis ate. This is a gumbo and this is a poke salad.

Mam   This is bloody ridiculous. Your dad doesn't want chitterlings or poke salad. He can barely even chew.

Jill   Well, I can liquidise it.

Mam   I'll bloody well liquidise you in a minute, Jilly. I want you to stop cooking these meals.

Jill   What are you on about?

Mam   All this weight you're putting on. Look at you, you're becoming obese.

Jill   Just because you never eat anything doesn't mean I'm becoming obese. Anyway, it's better than being an alcoholic.

Mam   Jilly, I am not an alcoholic.

Mam *takes a drink of wine.*

Jill   You drink all the time.

Mam   Don't be so stupid.

Jill   You want to watch it or you'll rot your liver. Look, you're doing it again.

Mam   Jill, it's the one bit of relaxation I get in this house. Anyway, it wouldn't surprise me if I had become an alcoholic living with him.

Jill   What's that supposed to mean?

Mam   You know quite nicely, Jill.

Jill   Are you referring to Dad?

Mam   I think we should just have a nice meal and then put him in his room.

Jill   I don't know what you are referring to, Mam?

Mam   Just forget it. It's his birthday.

Jill   At least he was nice to me. At least he wasn't pissed all the time.

Mam   Shut it or I'll clip you.

Jill   See, that's all you can think of, isn't it. Resorting to physical violence. I wish it was you who'd had the accident.

Mam   Jill, you have no idea what you are talking about. You seem to forget what I had to put up with with him. You seem to forget certain black eyes, certain trips to the RVI.

Jill   You probably deserved it.

Mam   Don't you dare talk to me like that.

Jill   I think you wanted him to be a disabled.

Mam   Are you out of your mind, Jill? Do you really think I want to be saddled with this for the rest of my life? Do you really think I'm enjoying myself? Jesus Christ.

Jill   Well, you seem to have plenty fun with your boyfriends.

Mam   Jill, I don't have any fun with my boyfriends.

Jill   That's ridiculous.

Mam   Look, all I want is some adult company once in a while.

Jill   You've got me.

Mam   Jill, you are a child.

Jill   No I'm not.

Mam   Gillian, you are a fat child. You should lose some weight and get yourself out from under my feet.

Jill   Mam, I'm not under your feet. I do everything. The cleaning. I do all the cooking, Mam.

Mam   I don't want your bloody cooking. Look, I'm just worried about you, that's all.

Jill   Why do you hate me, Mam?

Mam   I don't hate you. I don't hate him. I don't hate anyone. I hate myself. I'm going upstairs.

Jill   But you haven't eaten anything.

Mam   I've had quite sufficient, thank you very much.

Jill   Mam, it took ages.

Mam   I've told you, Gillian.

Jill   But Mam.

Mam   That's enough.

Mam *leaves.* **Jill** *starts to feed* **Dad**. *The gumbo dribbles down his chin.*

Jill   Great birthday party this has been.

Jill *kisses him.*

Lighting change so only the door is lit. **Dad** *is in darkness.*

Scene Six

Spot up on **Dad**. *He gets up and sings 'Burning Love'.*

Dad   'Oh, oh, oh. I feel my temperature rising.'

This is 'pissy' Elvis. It is like a bad club act. Perhaps there is taped applause at the end of the number. **Dad** *sits back in his chair and adopts his 'vegetable' position.* **Jill** *wheels him off.*

Scene Seven

Jill   Scene Seven. Some Days Later.

Jill *is sitting with a cookery book. The door opens.* **Stuart** *comes in with* **Mam**.

Mam   I'm glad you turned up. For a minute I didn't think you were going to show.

Stuart   Sorry. I had a bit of a problem with the Bakewell tarts.

Mam   You remember Gillian, don't you.

Stuart   Hiya.

Jill   Hello.

Mam   Jill was just off to do her homework.

Jill   No, I wasn't.

Mam   Yes you were, darling.

Jill *glares at* **Mam**, *then harrumphs out – giving them a hacky look.*

Mam   So, how are you?

Stuart   Well, I've been a bit busy, like. We've got a new line of lemon slices, so mostly I've been working nights.

Mam   Look, I just wanted to say that, well, I'm sorry, you know, about last time.

Stuart   Oh, there's no need to apologise.

Mam   I was just a little emotional.

Stuart   Really, it was nothing. I'm used to that sort of thing.

Mam   Really?

Stuart   Oh, yes. Epilepsy, that sort of thing. I've got a first-aid certificate as part of the training.

Mam   Well, you were very good about it.

Stuart   Divvint worry about it. I mean, I'm sorry about your husband being a cabbage and everything. You should have telt is.

Mam   It's not the kind of thing you like to talk about.

Stuart   Oh, it doesn't bother me. Is he here?

Mam   He's in the back. We had it built on with the insurance.

Stuart   Look. I brought you this.

Stuart *produces a small box.*

Mam   You shouldn't have. What is it?

Stuart   It's nothing really. Go on, open it.

Mam   Oh. Lovely. A cake.

Stuart   It's only a Victoria sponge.

Mam   Thanks anyway.

Stuart   It's the most popular line we do.

Mam   Really.

Stuart   Would you like to try some?

Mam   Maybe later. I'm watching my weight.

Stuart   I don't know why. You look fine to me.

Mam   That's because I watch my weight. Do you fancy a drink or something?

Stuart   I dunno. I suppose so.

Mam   Whisky all right?

Enter **Jill**.

Jill   Are you drinking already?

Mam   I thought you were doing your homework.

Jill   I'm finished.

Mam   You can't possibly be finished. You were only gone three minutes.

Jill   You can look at it if you want.

Mam   What about your project?

Jill   I can't do any more until I get the books I need.

Mam   She's doing a project. On food.

Jill   Gastronomy actually.

Mam   She's obsessed with food.

Jill   I am not obsessed.

Stuart   Well, I like a bit of food myself.

Jill   The project is on the philosophy of cooking.

Stuart   Philosophy.

Jill   Did you know in the eighteenth century people thought that meat would taste better if you tortured the animals before they were eaten?

Mam   Here's your Scotch.

Jill   They used to whip pigs to death with knotted ropes. And stamp on chickens.

Stuart   And they teach you that at school.

Jill   What?

Stuart   Chicken abuse.

Jill   No. You pick the subject yourself.

Stuart   I hated school, me.

Jill   Didn't you need GCSEs to be a supervisor?

Stuart   No, me uncle Harry sorted it out for me. I was crap at everything except games.

Mam   Stuart. I think it would be nice to go out and have a drink. Don't you think?

Stuart I'm all right here. Honest.

Jill He hasn't even finished his drink yet.

Mam I'll just go and get smartened up and we'll leave you to it, dear. I'll not be a minute.

Jill glowers at Mam as she goes out.

Jill Mam's a teacher, you know.

Stuart A teacher. I thought she worked somewhere part-time.

Jill That's right, a school.

Stuart She's not like a normal teacher.

Jill Perhaps you haven't met many normal teachers.

Stuart I mean, if there'd been more teachers like your mam at our school I might have paid more interest.

Jill So you didn't stay on, I take it.

Stuart There wasn't much point. Anyway, I don't think exams can tell you much. There's some managers at our place with degrees from university and they're as thick as pig shit.

Jill Mam went to university.

Stuart Well, I'm not saying everyone's as thick as pig shit.

Jill Do you think she's good-looking?

Stuart Who, your mam?

Jill Yeah.

Stuart She's a very attractive woman. For her age.

Jill She's an alcoholic, you know.

Stuart What do you mean?

Jill And an anorexic.

Stuart A what?

Jill   You know. Throws her food up and that.

Stuart   You'd never think to look at her.

Jill   So you don't think it's weird or anything.

Stuart   How do you mean?

Jill   Coming round here when Dad's a quadriplegic with head trauma.

Stuart   Well, it's quite weird.

Jill   So why have you come?

Stuart   I don't know. I wasn't going to. But your mam persuaded iz.

Jill   Maybe you haven't got much self-esteem.

Stuart   So your dad. Is he totally crippled?

Jill   Virtually. Though he does get erections.

Stuart   How do you know?

Jill   You can see them in his trousers. He gets them all the time. It got so embarrassing we stopped taking him into Safeway's.

Stuart   He got an erection in Safeway's.

Jill   I think he fancied the woman on Fruit and Veg.

Stuart   But how does he . . . you know . . . ?

Jill   What?

Stuart   Relieve himself?

Jill   He can't, can he. He's a cripple.

Stuart   What a shame.

Pause.

Jill   Stuart. Do you masturbate?

Stuart   I beg your pardon.

Jill   How often do you masturbate?

Stuart   I don't know. I've never kept count.

Jill   Apparently, the average British man masturbates four times a day.

Stuart   Well, I've never done it that much.

Jill   I thought you'd be at it all the time. Being a single man and everything.

Stuart   Look, this isn't really something I want to get into. Although I once caught a fella messing round in the almond slices.

Jill   What happened?

Stuart   He got promoted.

Jill   After masturbating in the almond slices.

Stuart   Well, it's not the type of thing you want getting out. We just kept him away from the batter.

Jill   So you're not married then?

Stuart   Me? No. I live with me mam, but she's moving into sheltered accommodation.

Jill   You want to be careful. Mam'll have you moving in here.

Stuart   What, with your dad and everything.

Jill   I told you she's mental.

Mam *comes back.* **Stuart** *looks worried.*

Mam   Well, I see you two are getting on like a house on fire.

Jill   We were just talking about my project.

Mam   Well, that's enough to put anybody off.

Scene Eight

Jill   Scene Eight. Elvis the Pelvis.

Spot comes up on **Dad***. Glitterball.* **Dad** *sings.*

Dad   You know, it ain't easy being King. I mean, things can sure get lonesome down here in old Graceland, there's all the pills I have to take, and all the records I have to do, and there's Pricilla going on and on, Jeez that girl's as uptight as a polecat's arse. Yes, sir. It sure can get lonesome. But say it's the afternoon, and I've been hard at it with my kung fu, or maybe I've been asleep, or maybe I've been lying down or maybe I'm just a bit blue. All I have to do is call Hamburger Joe. I just call him up and I say – Hamburger Joe, I say, boy, you better fix me some burgers and you better be a-gittin them quick. And before you can holler Poke Salad Annie that boy is outta that door and he's a-gittin me my burgers. Then they give me some pills or a little injection and they sit me up ready for the burgers. And then in come the burgers on the burger tray. Then first I take a burger and some dill pickle and then I eat them and then I have a Coke. Then I get another burger and I eat it and have a Coke. Then I eat another burger and some corn relish and then I have me a Doctor Pepper, and then I eat the mash potato and then I have a burger and then I have a Coke. Then sometimes I pass out. And then sometimes I have ice cream. It ain't always easy. But, I tell ya, it sure beats working for a living. Yes, suree.

Dad *gets back into his chair. A lighting change.* **Mam** *is beside him, a glass of Scotch in her hand.*

Scene Nine

Mam   Look, all I want you to know, Davey, is that I don't love him. I know we've . . . you know . . . had sex . . . a few times, but you understand that, don't you. I mean, I'm still a young woman, Davey, I still have needs, and I say we've had sex, but I mean he's just a young lad, Davey, he might go like the clappers but it's not what we had, Davey. I mean, I've never even sucked him off, except that once when we were watching *Neighbours*, but all I'm saying, Davey, it's just a way for me to stop losing those feelings for you. I mean, you wouldn't just want me to be barren, would you, Davey? You don't want me to become sour. But sometimes I need it, Davey, to just be held, so I forget, you know, just so I can remember what it's like, Davey. I look at us, and we're what? Thirty-eight years of age. What happened? I know we didn't always see eye to eye. But who would have expected this when you used to hold me so tight I could burst, when we had all those plans, Davey, of growing old together, of fixing things up, of being in love, Davey. So many things. What happened? Sometimes I just feel alone. You know, I'm still a young woman, Davey. I still want to laugh till it hurts and drink till I'm stupid and fuck till I'm numb and cry till I'm happy again, Davey, and be alive, I want to be alive.

Pause.

But it's the silence. The silence.

Jill *slowly comes in at the door.*

Jill   Mam.

Mam   I'm just talking to Dad.

Jill   What are you doing with the lights off?

Mam   Nothing.

Jill   Mam. Are you OK?

Mam   I'm drunk.

Jill   Mam.

Mam   And I don't give a shit.

Jill   Perhaps you should go to bed.

Mam   Why?

Jill   You've got school in the morning.

Mam   I'm not going to school in the morning.

Jill   Mam, you've got to. You're the teacher.

Mam   What's the point?

Jill   You know what the point is.

Mam   I am not going. The whole thing is fucking pointless, Jilly.

Jill   Mam. You have to stop this drinking.

Mam   Thirty-eight years of age and on the scrap heap.

They sit in silence.

Jill   I think it's time for his tablets.

Scene Ten

Breakfast. **Jill** *is eating a grapefriut.* **Mam** *takes a Diet Coke out of the fridge.*

Jill   Scene Ten. 'I can't believe you're drinking that.' I can't believe you're drinking that.

Mam   What's wrong with this?

Jill   Diet Coke. For breakfast?

Mam   There's nothing wrong with that.

Jill   Mam, it's not good for you. It can make you fat.

Mam   Diet Coke? It hasn't got any calories.

Jill   Mam, it's the chemicals. Aspartame and that. There are all these people in America who've swollen up like balloons.

Mam   Jill, in case you hadn't noticed. I am not fat.

Jill   Well, why are you drinking Diet Coke then?

Mam Jill, this food business is getting out of hand.

Jill Don't talk to me about things getting out of hand.

Mam It's obsessive. It isn't healthy.

Jill It's not healthy to throw your food up but I'm not complaining.

Mam Jill, you have a problem.

Jill You're the one with the problem. You're the one who's moved your stupid boyfriend in, when Dad is just next door.

Mam Jill. He is not my boyfriend.

Jill Well, what's he doing living here then?

Mam He had nowhere to stay, Jilly. We've been through this.

Jill Well, what are you screwing him for if he's not your boyfriend?

Mam Don't start.

Jill You should only sleep with people if you really love them.

Mam It's not that simple, sweetheart.

Jill Well, what's the point of sleeping with him if you don't love him?

Mam Jilly, there are things I need.

Jill Have you thought about what Dad thinks?

Mam He doesn't think anything. He doesn't know what's going on.

Jill He might.

Mam With the medication he's on he doesn't know whether he's coming or going.

Jill But what if he does know?

Mam   What if he does? What difference would it make?

Jill   Mam, what you need is to stop being horrible.

Mam   What you need is to get yourself out more. Get yourself a boyfriend before you're too fat to get out of the front door.

Jill   So basically all you want is for me to be a slut like you.

Mam   Listen, if it makes you a more pleasant human being, frankly I'd be delighted.

Jill   Mam. I hate you. And the stupid cake man.

Stuart *walks in in his pyjamas.*

Stuart   Morning.

They both look at **Stuart**.

Scene Eleven

Jill   Scene Eleven. Trivial Pursuits.

Jill *goes out leaving* **Mum** *and* **Stuart**.

Mam *and* **Stuart** *are playing Trivial Pursuits.*

Mam   A green piece of pie, please.

Stuart   Look, can we stop now?

Mam   What do you mean, we haven't even finished.

Stuart   But it's hypothetical. I haven't even got a bit of pie.

Mam   Play the game, Stuart.

Stuart   It's just I wanted to talk to you seriously.

Mam   What on earth do you want to talk seriously about?

Stuart   I mean, do you really think this is all right?

Mam   What do you mean all right?

Stuart It just seems a bit weird.

Mam Look. Your mam had to go into sheltered accommodation and there's more than enough room here. Come on.

Stuart Geography. What are the cannibal tribes of Borneo known as?

Mam Shit.

Stuart But what about Jill?

Mam What about her? She wants to mind her own business.

Stuart But I don't think she likes it.

Mam Of course she likes it. Christ, it's like a bloody mortuary with just the two of us. I think you've brought a bit of spice into our lives, Stuart.

Stuart Are you sure it's not weird or anything? I mean you're a teacher.

Mam Stuart. Teachers have lives, you know. Teachers have sex. Anyway, I didn't ask you to move in here because of your mind, Stuart.

Stuart Didn't you?

Mam The Dyaks.

Stuart I beg your pardon.

Mam The Dyaks of Borneo. Another piece of pie, please.

Stuart But I was thinking. Look, I'm just ordinary sweet goods supervision manager. It's just all a bit sudden.

Mam Look, Stuart. You could come out of your little cake factory tonight and get run over by a bus.

Stuart I just don't know if it's right. I mean. It was all right coming round now and again. But living with him.

Mam   Fuck him, Stuart. Fuck you and your stupid ideas of what's proper behaviour. All I want is to come home and not have to sit with him stinking of formaldehyde. All I want is to have a drink. Watch the telly. Just be normal. Just forget. There's nothing weird about that, is there?

Stuart   No.

Mam   Can't you see how important this is. To have you here.

Stuart   So you don't want me to move out or anything.

Mam   You've got the run of the place. What more do you want?

Stuart   It's just I don't know where I stand. With him and everything.

Mam   Stuart. You don't stand anywhere. You don't have to think about anything. All you have to do is stop your whinging and be here for me. It's not a lot to ask. Is it?

Stuart   I don't suppose so.

Mam *comes over to him seductively.*

Mam   Don't worry, Stuart, you can do anything you want with me. I'll make sure you know which side your bread's buttered on.

Stuart   Really?

He grabs a card to deflect the amorous attentions.

History. Which historical figure gave their cook a city?

Jill *is in chef's hat standing with Stanley watching. She puts him down and comes upstage to make something extremely delicate – like icing-sugar roses or something like that. Dad is onstage through the next scene. He starts to get an erection.*

Scene Twelve

Jill   Scene Twelve. A speech about cooking. In the olden
days they used to think that cooking was something special.
Mark Antony once gave his cook a whole city cos Cleopatra
liked his gravy. Those were the days when they really
appreciated things. They went all over the world to get stuff
to eat. Fantastic ingredients from all over the world.
Camels' feet cooked in roses. Whole plates of nightingales'
tongues, pigs that when you carved them doves would fly
out, marinaded lentils wrapped in gold. You see, they
appreciated food and it was good to be fat. It was sexy to be
fat. When you see them old paintings of women in the nude
– they weren't skinny, were they? They had something to be
proud of. Big pink tummies, enormous soft thighs and they
were always stuffing themselves with a bunch of grapes.
Sometimes I have this dream, where I'm lying there in the
middle of an enormous bowl of fruit, and I'm lying there in
the kiwis and papayas, totally naked, eating chocolate
puddings. I suppose, in that way, I'm quite old-fashioned,
really. And when I grow up that's what I want to be, Dad. A
cook and I'd have a husband who was a gourmet and we'd
live in a little cottage with hams hanging from the rafters
and every day we'd make the most exquisite recipes known
to man. And you'd be there too. In the back. And we'd pass
through your stuff through a little hatch in the wall.
Delicious delicacies that'd we'd pass through to your bit.
And then we'd be happy, Dad. Wouldn't we? Wouldn't we?

Jill *is in her bedroom. A few cuddly toys and cookery books.*

We hear a door close downstairs.

Stuart *(off)* Anybody home?

Jill *ignores this.*

Stuart   Anybody home?

Scene Thirteen

Jill   Scene Thirteen. The act-one twist. I'm upstairs.

Jill *continues reading. We hear* **Stuart** *come upstairs. he pops his head round the door.*

Stuart   Hija.

Jill   She's not in.

Stuart   When will she be back?

Jill   Dunno. She went to see Marg in Middlesbrough.

Stuart   What are you up to?

Jill   Nothing.

Stuart   Christ. You've got plenty books mind.

Jill   I collect them. What's that?

Stuart   What's what?

Jill   There?

Stuart   Oh. It's nothing. Here, you can have it.

Jill   Isn't it for Mam?

Stuart   I thought you'd prefer it.

Jill   Thanks.

Stuart   Well, open it.

Jill   It's a cake, isn't it.

Stuart   Not just any cake.

Jill   It's a Black Forest gateau.

Stuart   It's the fanciest one we do.

Jill   You nick these cakes, don't you?

Stuart   No one notices.

Jill   Did you really bring it here for me?

Stuart   Well, I thought you'd appreciate it.

Jill   Thanks.

Embarrassed silence.

Stuart   So how are you getting on at school?

Jill   All right.

Stuart   Get that project finished?

Jill   Nearly.

Stuart   Champion.

Jill   You can sit down if you like.

Stuart   No. It's all right. I mean, I just brought you the cake.

Jill   Stuart. How old are you?

Stuart   Twenty-six. Why like?

Jill   I just wondered why you were going out with a thirty-eight-year-old.

Stuart   Age doesn't matter. Anyway, when I met your mam I thought she was younger than me.

Jill   You were pissed.

Stuart   Still, it's the person that counts.

Jill   But isn't it more normal that a man goes out with someone younger than the other way round?

Stuart   So?

Jill   I'm just saying.

Stuart   Have you got a boyfriend?

Jill   I'm not really interested.

Stuart   It's not a crime, you know. Having a boyfriend.

Jill   I think I scare people off.

Stuart   Rubbish. You're dead easy to talk to.

Jill   Do you think?

Stuart   Yeah. Easier than your mam.

Jill   Lads my age aren't really into conversations.

Stuart   But you're quite attractive. You've got lovely bushy hair.

Jill   Have I?

Stuart   Yeah. It's the first thing I noticed about you, your hair. I wish I had hair like that.

Jill   Like mine?

Stuart   Well, a bit shorter, but you know.

Jill   I'm not exactly God's gift, am I?

Stuart   I wouldn't say that.

Jill   Mam's right, isn't she? I'm overweight.

Stuart   You're not overweight. Anyway, I prefer a bit of meat on somebody.

Jill   Serious?

Stuart   Course I'm serious.

Jill   Do you think I've got an attractive body?

Stuart   I think your body's very attractive.

Jill   Thanks.

Stuart   You're a very attractive person.

Jill   So are you.

Stuart   Really.

Jill   Would you like a bit of cake?

Stuart   You're all right for now. I thought you hated me.

Jill   I thought you hated me.

Stuart   No, I like you. I mean. You're a nice person. A caring person.

Jill   Not especially.

Stuart   Well, I mean, you're more of a caring person than say, your mam.

Jill   I thought you liked Mam.

Stuart   I do.

Jill   Well?

Stuart   All I'm saying is I feel comfortable with you. It's just nice to be able to have a chat now and again.

Jill   Do you think I'm as good-looking as Mam?

Stuart   Perhaps I'd better leave you to it.

Jill   No. You don't have to go.

Stuart   Really.

Jill   I don't mind. I like a bit of company.

Stuart *sits down.* **Jill** *eats a piece of cake.*

Stuart   You know your dad. What exactly did he do?

Jill   He used to be a surveyor, but he gave it up for entertainment.

Stuart   What sort of entertainment?

Jill   He used to be Elvis.

Stuart   Elvis Presley.

Jill   No, Elvis O'Connor. Who did you think?

Stuart   Christ.

Jill   I know.

Stuart   Do you not like Elvis, like?

Jill   I hate it. I still play it for him but it drives me mental.

Stuart   So he used to dress up and that.

Jill   Course. All his stuff's in there.

Stuart   You kept all his costumes and that?

Jill   Do you want a look?

Stuart   Sure. So what happened to him, like.

Jill   Who?

Stuart   Your dad.

Jill   His car hit a lorry and he went through the window. He'd only got round the corner. Everyone thought he was dead.

Stuart   Christ. He had plenty of gear then.

Jill   He used to do it every night.

Stuart   Look at this.

Jill   Try it on.

Stuart   You must be joking.

Jill   Go on. It'd look good on you.

Stuart   He must have been pretty serious about it.

Jill   I suppose.

Stuart   But he didn't think he actually was Elvis or anything.

Jill   You'd probably have to believe you're Elvis, wouldn't you. A bit.

Stuart   Would you?

Jill   To make it convincing.

Stuart   You reckon.

Jill   Everybody pretends they're someone else to make themselves more convincing. That's a fact of life.

Stuart   Is it?

Jill   Try it on.

Stuart   It's a bit weird, isn't it. With him being crippled and everything.

Jill   It's only a costume.

Stuart   All right then. As long as you don't tell your mam.

He starts to change and then gets self-conscious.

What are you looking at me like that for?

Jill   I'm just watching.

Stuart   You're a right bunch of perverts, you.

Jill   And the pants.

Stuart   Are you sure?

Jill   Go on. Look. They fit perfect.

Stuart   They're a bit tight round here.

Jill   They're supposed to be.

Stuart   What do you reckon?

Jill   You look great.

Stuart   Do you think I'm sexy?

Jill   What do you mean?

Stuart   You know, do I turn you on as Elvis?

Jill   I don't know.

Stuart   I've seen you look at iz.

Jill   Looking like what?

Stuart   Like you were interested.

Jill   In what?

Stuart   How old are you?

Jill   What difference does that make?

Stuart   Not a lot.

Jill   Why did you ask?

Stuart   I was just interested.

Jill   Fourteen.

Stuart   Do you usually invite strange men to get changed in your bedroom.

Jill   You're not a strange man.

Stuart   Am I not?

Jill   Not to me.

Stuart   What would your mother think?

Jill   I don't know.

Stuart   Do you not think she'd get the wrong impression with me in this suit and everything?

Jill   Maybes she'd think it was perfectly natural.

Stuart   Natural.

Jill   I don't see what's wrong with it.

Stuart   Really.

Jill   You look good in that suit.

Stuart   Maybe I should take it off now.

Jill   Maybe you should leave it on.

Stuart   Won't your mother be back.

Jill   She'll be at least another hour.

Stuart   Will she indeed.

Jill   Do you think I should put a record on?

Stuart   As long as it's Elvis Presley.

Jill *starts to go.* **Stuart** *grabs her arm. They kiss.*

Stuart   Do you really think we should be doing this.

Jill   I don't see why not.

They kiss again.

Elvis comes out of the wardrobe singing 'The Wonder of You'. Maybe he gets covered in dry ice and when it has cleared, he has disappeared and they are in the bed.

Scene Fourteen

Jill *appears on the bed standing up,* **Stuart** *on top of her, as if it's a bird's-eye view.*

Jill   Scene Fourteen. A Speech about Gravy.

Jill *is being fucked by* **Stuart**. *She has a slice of cake that she nibbles on intermittently.*

Dad, I'm only telling you this because you won't tell anyone else. Look, even if you do get better you have to promise not to tell anyone. At all. You see, yesterday, I did it with someone. I mean, I didn't mean to. I mean, it's all right to have it off with someone even if you don't love them. Isn't it? I mean, you had it off with that woman from Tynemouth, didn't you, and you didn't love her. Did you? But the thing was, Dad, even though it was all right and that, even though I quite enjoyed it, well, it felt weird. Like I shouldn't be doing it. I could feel all this cold polyester against my leg and all I could think of was you. The sequins were sticking into me and all I could think of was you and Mam and Grandma. And I kept looking over to the wardrobe, and all the time he was on iz, all that I could think of was that Mam would jump out. That everyone would jump out of the wardrobe, Mam, Grandma, the cookery teacher, everybody. And they would catch iz, Dad. And he was kissing iz. And he was all hot. Smoky breath and his fly was like cutting into me leg. And I felt terrible, and all I could think of was you. And then I started to smell this smell, and the smell was this sweet smell of dough. And then I thought of a big plate of dumplings. Then I imagined Mam and she was eating the dumplings. And she was sitting there eating the dumplings and she was crying. And I was passing her the gravy and she was eating the dumplings. And he was saying she loved iz. And I didn't know what to do, Dad. And all I could think of was big sticky dumplings and gravy. Thick, salty gravy.

Stuart *is finished, zips himself up and leaves.* **Jill** *tidies herself up.*

Scene Fifteen

Kitchen. **Jill** *is cooking up a storm.*

Jill   Scene Fifteen. The Kitchen.

Mam   Jill.

Jill   Hang on a minute, Mam. I'm busy.

Mam   Jill, stop cooking.

Jill   I can't stop now or it'll be spoilt.

Mam   Jill, I said stop cooking. I want a word with you, young lady.

Jill   What's the matter now?

Mam   I need to talk to you. Look, sit down. It's something personal.

Jill   Have I done something wrong?

Mam   Look, Jill, I don't want you to think I've been snooping round or anything.

Jill   What have you been doing?

Mam   Jilly, there's something I just don't understand.

Jill   Mam, if you've been in my room.

Mam Jill, I wasn't snooping around.

Jill What were you doing in there?

Mam I was cleaning up, Jilly.

Jill You've got no right to go in there.

Mam Jill, I have to talk to you about this.

She produces a bag which she holds at arm's length. **Jill** *blanches.*

I was so disgusted I have had to put it in a plastic bag.

Jill Mam, I can explain.

Mam But it was under your bed.

Jill There's an explanation.

Mam What the hell is going on, Jill?

Jill It was fermenting.

Mam Fermenting, Jilly, this is a salted fish.

Jill They need a cool dark place.

Mam It's disgusting.

Jill It's Vietnamese.

Mam Look, it's absolutely fetid.

Jill That's how it's supposed to be.

Mam I'm at the end of my tether here.

Jill I won't do it again.

Mam It's OK to keep these things in the kitchen, Jill. But no more food in your bedroom. It's absolutely unhygienic.

Jill I'm sorry, Mam. I better carry on.

Mam You don't have to do this, you know. I don't know why you're insisting on cooking for Stuart.

Jill Mam, I want to.

Mam   I know it's very nice of you. But you don't have to do it all the time, darling.

Jill   Mam, I want to. It's a labour of love.

Scene Sixteen

Stuart, **Jill**, **Mam** *and* **Dad** *all sit down at the table.*

Jill   Scene Sixteen. Things Turn Nasty. What do you think?

Stuart   It's a nice bit of fish this.

Jill   It's sole veronique.

Stuart   I never thought grapes would go. Are you not eating any?

Mam   I've had plenty. It's quite rich, isn't it?

Jill   No, it's not rich at all. Is it, Stuart?

Stuart   No. I mean yes. I mean, it's just very nice, isn't it?

Jill   Don't you think it's weird how Mam hardly eats anything?

Stuart   Well, she's watching her weight, isn't she? She wants to look attractive.

Jill   You don't have to watch your weight to be attractive though, do you. I thought you said you liked a bit of meat on somebody.

Mam   When did you say that?

Stuart   I don't know. Maybe I mentioned it in passing.

Mam   Anyway, I think that's right. Don't you think she looks attractive in the new dress I bought her?

Stuart   Yes, she looks very nice.

Mam   See. If you got yourself a new haircut, you could start attracting the fellas.

Jill   Mam, I think you should change the subject.

Mam   Why?

Jill   Cos Stuart doesn't want to hear about me.

Mam   Course he does. You're interested in Jilly, aren't you?

Stuart   Yes. I mean . . .

Mam   Don't you think if she just lost a couple of pounds she'd look great?

Stuart   She does look great.

Mam   But don't you think they'd be going wild for her if she was just a bit trimmer?

Stuart   Mam. Will you shut up.

Mam   I was just asking Stuart's opinion.

Stuart   Anyway, I think it's the person that counts not what they look like.

Jill   Do you think I'm not good-looking?

Stuart   Of course I think you're good-looking. I was just saying.

Jill   Look, if you don't think I'm attractive just say so.

Mam   All we're saying, Jilly, if you lost a few pounds you'd be even more attractive.

Jill   Is that what you're saying?

Stuart   I'm not saying anything.

Mam   I don't know why you're flying off the handle. I'm just trying to give you some friendly advice.

Jill   I don't want your advice. You're the one he doesn't find attractive.

Mam   What on earth are you on about? Do you find me unattractive?

Stuart   Course not.

Mam   So what are you on about?

Jill   Mam. Basically, you are just ignorant.

Mam   Sit down.

Jill   Oh, piss off, Mam.

Mam   Gillian.

Jill   I'm taking him through, you can clear up, the pair of yous.

Jill *storms off, sticking a lump of food in her gob as she goes.*

Mam   I don't know what's got into her.

Stuart   Maybe I should go and talk to her.

Mam   Fuck her, if that's how she's going to be. Stuart, I want you inside of me.

Stuart   I beg your pardon.

Mam   Right here. On the table.

Stuart   In the middle of the fish and everything.

Mam   Fuck me, Stuart.

Stuart   But what about me trousers?

Mam   For Christ's sake. That'll do nicely, Stuart.

Mam *grabs* **Stuart** *on to the table. They make love. Mam grabs* **Stuart**'s *head and thrusts it down to her crotch. Crossfade to* **Jill** *and* **Dad** *upstage. We hear the burbled orgasmic noises coming from the kitchen table as if they were in another room.*

Scene Seventeen

Silence.

Jill   I didn't know you could hear so much through here.

Suddenly **Dad** *comes out of the wheelchair in Elvis gear and sings 'Suspicious Minds' with great aplomb.*

The stage is cleared. Then it plunges into darkness. Pitch black. The bedroom door opens. **Mam** *appears in her dressing gown. She is going to the loo. She suddenly sees* **Jill**. *She gets a shock.*

Scene Eighteen

Jill   Scene Eighteen. The Landing. Night.

Mam   What are you doing here?

Jill   I couldn't sleep.

Mam   You haven't been cooking, have you?

Jill   No.

Mam   What's that smell?

Jill   It's nothing. It's from before. I was looking for Stanley.

Mam   Jill, it's half past three in the morning. Go to bed.

Jill   Mam, do you think Stuart loves you?

Mam   Let's not get into that again. Go to bed, darling, I need the loo.

Jill   But do you?

Mam   This is neither the time nor the place.

Jill   But Mam . . .

Mam   Jilly, this is ridiculous.

Jill   Mam, I've got something to tell you.

Mam   What is it?

Jill   Mam. I've got a boyfriend.

Mam   That's wonderful, darling, is it anyone I know?

Jill   No.

Mam   I know exactly how you feel. It's perfectly normal not to be able to sleep. But really you should be in bed now. Take Stanley to your room if it makes you feel better.

Jill   Mam, do you love Stuart?

Mam   It's the middle of the night.

Jill   But how do you know if somebody really loves you?

Mam   You can just tell. Good night.

Jill   Good night, Mam.

Mam *goes to the loo.* **Jill** *then reappears and opens the bedroom door.*

Jill   Stuart. Stuart.

Stuart *appears at the door almost naked and pushes* **Jill** *into the corridor.*

Stuart   Jesus Christ. You can't come in here.

Jill   Stuart. I need to talk to you.

Stuart   Do you know what time it is?

Jill   It's the middle of the night.

Stuart   What do you want?

Jill   I want you, Stuart.

Stuart   Jesus Christ. Your mam's only gone to have a slash.

Jill   I don't care.

Stuart   Jesus.

Jill   You hardly looked at me all night.

Stuart   What do you expect?

Jill   I thought you loved me.

Stuart   I never said I loved you.

Jill   Yes, you did.

Stuart   Look, what's happened between us has been a big mistake.

Jill   What do you mean a mistake?

Stuart   I just got carried away.

Jill   But you said you loved me.

Stuart   Keep your voice down. I never meant to say that. It just came out.

Jill   Came out.

Stuart   Oh, I don't know. It's just what you say.

Jill   But I love you.

Stuart   No you don't. Look, you're a lovely kid but . . .

The toilet flushes.

Jill   Kid! I'm your lover.

Stuart   For God's sake, you're still at school.

Jill   Well, you had it off with me.

Stuart   She'll be out in a second.

Jill   Look, I've made you these.

Stuart   What the hell are they?

Jill   They're truffles. They've got your name on.

Stuart   Look, take them back, I don't want them.

Jill   They're a present.

Stuart   Look, this has to stop.

Mam *comes out.*

Stuart   Shit.

Jill   Well, stuff you then.

Jill *gives the truffles to* **Stuart** *and disappears.*

Mam   What are you doing?

Stuart   I was just going to the toilet.

Mam   What are you doing with those?

Stuart   I was just a bit peckish.

Mam *goes past and trips.*

Mam   That bloody tortoise. Put those down and come back to bed.

She closes the door. **Jill** *reappears.*

Jill   Stuart, I want you. Now.

Stuart   For Christ's sake.

Jill   Come on, we can go into the bathroom.

Stuart   Look, this is getting completely out of hand.

Jill   It's all right. Just bring the truffles.

Stuart   Jill, we are not going anywhere. This has to stop. I don't love you. Our relationship is going nowhere. Understand. Finito.

Mam *opens the door.*

Mam   What are you two up to?

Jill   I'm still looking for Stanley.

Mam   Get to bed at once, young lady. He's in my room because I nearly crippled myself with him running round the landing.

Jill *goes off.*

Mam And for God's sake put those sweets down.

She goes back inside and stubs her toe on Stanley.

Ow! That fucking tortoise.

Stuart *is left alone.* **Jill** *reappears and grabs the truffles.*

Jill I hate you.

Jill *storms off.*

Stuart Fucking hell.

Dad *as Elvis appears on the balcony.*

Dad It happened the first time when I was in Vegas and Priscilla was wearing her skin-tight, velour catsuit, it happened the second time in Phoenix when I was in the jacuzzi with the little fox from Reno. It happened at home in Graceland after breakfast. And I called for the doctor and I asked him, Doc, how can this be that the King who has all the riches of this world, all the girls he could dream of, I asked him, Doc, what could be wrong now, why do I have this erectile disfunction. And the doc said, son, you maybe the King, you may have Cadillacs and all kinds of foxy minxes, but son, all around you is despair, poverty, hurt and suffrin, and you must feel for them all. You must feel for the poor, the mean, the harelipped and the ugly, the sad, the dejected, the wounded and heartbroken and sodomites. Sodomites rutting in cornfields and in greyhound buses, in airplanes, on doorsteps, wiping their dirty little organs on the lily-white paper of our constitution. He said, son, it ain't no surprise you have that erectile disfunction, with all that weight on your poor shoulders. This ain't an easy time for any of us, and it ain't an easy time to be King.

Dad *disappears.*

Jill *alone. She takes the pie out of the oven in a demonic state. And prepares the meal for the next scene.*

Scene Nineteen

Jill   Scene Nineteen. Mr Kipling gets his Fucking Pie.

Jill *looks awful.* **Mam** *and* **Stuart** *sit down to eat.*

Stuart   Hiya.

Jill   Hiya.

Mam   Are you all right, Jill?

Jill   Fine.

Mam   You look a bit tired, that's all.

Jill   I'm absolutely fine, Mam.

Mam   Well, this looks lovely, doesn't it, Stuart?

Stuart   Oh yeh, I like a nice bit of pie.

Mam   It's got an unusual smell.

Jill   It's African.

Mam   That's very original.

Stuart   I've never had anything African before.

Jill   I thought I'd try something different.

Stuart   Well, it's quite tasty actually.

Jill   I'm not sure if it was a good idea. Mam, I'm starting to go off food.

Mam   Well, that's good.

Jill   I mean, it's terrible what people eat, isn't it?

Stuart   What do you mean?

Jill   Like tripe is sheep's stomach and black puddings are blood.

Stuart   Black puddings are lovely though.

Jill   Well, sheep's eyes and monkeys' brains.

Stuart   You're putting me right off.

Jill   And chicken's feet and woodlice and sperm.

Mam   Jilly. People do not eat sperm.

Jill   People do eat sperm. Cod roe.

Mam   Cod roe is fish eggs, darling.

Jill   But soft roe is sperm, Mam. Sperm from a fish.

Mam   Is there anything wrong, sweetheart?

Jill   No.

Mam   You seem a bit tense.

Jill   I'm fine.

Mam   How's this boyfriend of yours getting on?

Jill   OK.

Mam   Has something happened?

Jill   No.

Mam   Are you sure?

Jill   He's a complete bastard.

Mam   Well, it's all in the process of learning, dear.

Jill   I hate him, Mam, and I hate all the tortes and the omelettes and the custards and the stews and the puddings. All that chopping and pummelling and mincing, everything that's mashed and smashed and ripped apart. Mam, it's not natural, it's worse than animals. It's disgusting. We're all disgusting, Mam, human beings. I hate everything, every stupid last thing I ever wanted to cook for him.

Mam   What on earth's been going on, Jill.

Jill   It's like I saw all the things I've eaten. You know all the things that were alive and sudddenly I felt rotten. I mean, I thought what if there was something inside of me. No bigger than a pea. How would I like it if someone put

that on a pizza? And then I thought about the Third World
and all the starving children in Africa and there is Kate
Moss without an ounce of fat to rub together. And I thought
about all this and I just felt sick.

Mam   What do you mean there was something inside of
you?

Jill   It was just something I thought.

Stuart   Maybe I should leave you alone.

Jill   Stay there.

Mam   What do you mean, Jill?

Jill   I don't know.

Mam   Have you been messing around with this boyfriend
of yours, Jill?

Jill   No.

Mam   What's wrong, Jill?

Jill   I thought he loved me. He said that he loved me.

Mam   Who is this boy, Jill?

Jill   It's not a boy.

Mam   Jesus. It's not that Mary from across the road, is it?

Jill   It's a man.

Mam   A man. What sort of man?

Jill   I don't know.

Mam   Well, did you use protection?

Jill   I don't know.

Mam   What do you mean you don't know? How old is he,
Jill?

Jill   I don't know. Stuart's age.

Mam   Stuart's age. Where on earth did you meet such a man?

Jill   I don't know.

Mam   Jill, this is serious.

Jill   What's serious about it? It's all right for you to sleep around.

Mam   I don't sleep around.

Jill   What about him?

Mam   Stuart and I have a relationship.

Jill   Well, so do I.

Mam   What?

Jill   Have a relationship. You think you're perfect sitting there all high and mighty looking down on me and everything. But you're the one to blame. Look what you did to Dad. But you won't admit it. You don't even care. You've got no conscience at all, have you? You're just a bastard.

Mam   All I do is have a conscience, Jill. I wake up every bloody morning and it's all I think about. What if we hadn't have argued. What if I'd never said I was leaving. What if. What if. But he did it, Jill. He was the one like a bat out of hell. I didn't ask him to. And what's worse is when I went round there and he was lying there, there was part of me that thought, it serves you right, you fucking bastard. It serves you right. Imagine how that makes me feel. All I do is have a fucking conscience. So get off my back.

Stuart   Perhaps I should leave yous to it.

Jill   Mam. I cooked Stanley in the pie.

Mam   You did what?

Stuart   For Christ's sake.

Mam   Gillian.

Stuart   You're fucking mental, you.

Jill   No, I'm not mental.

Stuart   You're off your dot.

Mam   Shut your mouth, son.

Stuart   I feel sick.

Mam   Just sit down there and shut your mouth before I shut it for you. What's going on, Jill?

Jill   I'm going to the toilet.

Mam   You're not going anywhere.

Stuart   Jill . . .

Jill   I don't give a shit about you any more.

Jill *glares at* **Stuart** *and then runs out.* **Mam** *follows.*

Stuart   Jesus Christ.

Jill *comes back on to announce, briefly.*

Jill   Scene Twenty. A Paranoid Speech by Elvis.

Scene Twenty

Dad *in spotlight as Elvis.*

Dad   You know it was never easy being King. There are bad and evil things in this world of mine. There is misery and there is pain but I was born to bring my people hope. So one day when I woke up and Priscilla was going on about me buying those ten Mercedes-Benz – and I just said, Priscilla, for gawd's sake shut up. What does my personal finance matter when there is a pestilence upon this nation. There is drugs and sodomising. This is no place for free men. And I said as America's number one American I'm going to see me the President. So I put on my Elvis cape and my Elvis belt and I caught the plane to Washington.

And then at the airport I saw this nigger sitting. And I said, boy, take me to see the President. And he said, ain't you the King. And I said, keep it under your hat, boy, cos this gun's undercover. And we went off to the White House by way of Dunkin Donuts where I had a couple o' dozen cos I'd dun missed my breakfast. And then the President came out and he said: Gee, Elvis, you sure wear some wayout clothing. And I said to the President, Mr President, sir, you've got your show to run and I got mine. And I said, Mr President, there is a pestilence upon this kingdom. My people are walking in a valley of woe. There is a darkness upon us. There's drugs and hippies and sodomites and every kind of evil. But where there is sadness I will bring hope, and where there is sorrow I will bring love, and where there is poverty I will bring the riches of the Orient, and where there is darkness I will bring light, and where there is hunger I will bring burgers. And all will be well and all manner of things will be well. And then I went home and was sick.

Dad *sits back down in his chair and adopts his comatose position.*

Jill *wheels him into position.*

Scene Twenty-One

Jill   Scene Twenty-One. Quite Near the Ending.

Stuart comes in and sits next to him.

Dad *is in his chair. He has an erection.* **Stuart** *comes over to him, takes out his dick and starts to toss him off.*

Stuart   Look, I know this must seem really weird, me wanting to talk to you and everything. But I just felt I had to, you know. I've got nobody else. And I know you must be thinking who's this bastard coming here seeing wor lass and the young un as well. But I never did it out of spite or nowt. I mean, I know I shouldn't have fucked the bairn. But she doesn't seem like a kid to me. I mean, in a way I thought I might be falling in love, you know.

Sorry, me hand's getting a bit sore. And I just want you to know like. I don't usually mess about with blokes, like. I'm only doing this because you're a cripple. And I just want you to know. I mean, even though I've been fucking your wife and everything. I want you to know you have my upmost respect. I mean, I wouldn't be doing this if I didn't respect you. And they love you. And they're both yours, you know that. I've fucked it now. I've got nobody, me.

Dad *comes all over* **Stuart**'*s hand.*

Stuart   There you go.

He wipes his hand on **Dad**'*s costume. A little bit is left.* **Stuart** *is curious. He sniffs the hand and then tastes a little bit of* **Dad**'*s cum. He thinks. He bends over, holds* **Dad**'*s head up and kisses him on the mouth.*

Jill *comes in.*

Jill   What are you doing?

Stuart   Nowt.

Jill   You were kissing me dad.

Stuart   No I wasn't. I was just giving him his medicine.

Jill   His medicine. Look at the state of him. What have you been doing?

Stuart   I haven't done anything.

Jill   I've had enough of you, you bastard. What have you been doing?

Stuart   I wanked him off.

Jill   You did what?

Stuart   He got an erection and I wanked him off.

Jill   Who do you think you are coming in here fucking me mother, shagging me, wanking me dad off. It's a good job I killed the fucking tortoise. I loved you. You fucking bastard.

Stuart It wasn't what you think.

Jill Wasn't what I think. A wank is a wank, Stuart. And you're the biggest fucking wanker I've ever laid eyes on.

Stuart Hey. Don't call me a wanker.

Jill You're sick. Get him out of here, take him next door.

Stuart Look, stop ordering me around.

Jill Do you want me to tell Mam? Eh.

Stuart Listen . . .

Jill What do you think she'll say when she finds out you've fucked her daughter and wanked her husband off.

Stuart Look, there's nothing wrong with wanking your dad off.

Jill You're out of your mind.

Stuart They do it in the hospitals.

Jill Well, two can play at that game, matey.

Stuart Just calm down.

Jill If everybody else is getting wanked off left, right and centre I don't see why should be left out.

Stuart Look, Jilly, this has to stop right now.

Jill Take off your clothes.

Stuart What?

Jill I mean it, take them off.

Stuart You must be joking.

Jill I'm serious.

Stuart Your mam's upstairs.

Jill She's gone out.

Stuart But . . .

Jill   I want to fuck you on the table.

Stuart   Hang on a minute.

Jill   One last time and I'll never tell a living soul.

Stuart   But it's out of the question.

Jill   So you want me to tell her, do you?

Stuart   No. Jesus, no. But this is ridiculous.

Jill   Take your clothes off or I'll phone her now, she's at me nan's.

Stuart   This is ridiculous. Look, what about your dad?

Jill   Fuck me dad. I mean it. You could go to jail for what you did to me. Take your clothes off, Stuart.

Stuart   Look, one last time and that's that, OK?

Jill   Hurry up, she'll be back shortly.

Stuart *takes his clothes off. Down to his Y-fronts.*

Jill   Now get on the table.

Stuart   What's this?

Jill   I want you to rub it all over.

Stuart   But what is it?

Jill   It's a marinade. Rub it on you. Or else.

Stuart   You're a fucking pervert you.

Jill *pulls out a big kitchen knife.*

Jill   Rub it all over.

Stuart *looks at the knife, then at the jar and starts to rub on the marinade. Suddenly, we hear the door.* **Stuart** *starts.*

Jill   Stay there, you bastard.

Stuart   What are you going to do to me?

Jill   I'm going to fuck you good and proper.

Stuart   Please, put the knife down.

Jill   All over.

Stuart   Please, you're going too far.

Jill   You haven't a clue how far I'll go.

Mam (*off*)   Jilly!

She comes in.

What on earth is going on here?

Jill   Nothing.

Mam   What on earth are you doing?

Stuart   Look, I can explain.

Mam   What the hell is that stuff?

Jill   Marinade.

Mam   Jesus Christ. How long has this been going on?

Stuart   I think you've got the wrong idea.

Mam   How could you do this to me, Stuart?

Stuart   It wasn't on purpose.

Mam   What on earth were you thinking of?

Stuart   The whole thing was an accident.

Mam   An accident with that tub of lard?

Stuart   I'm sorry. Look, I'll go now. I'll never come back again.

Mam   Jesus Christ, Jilly.

Jill   Don't touch me. Leave me alone.

Jill *runs out.*

Stuart   Look, I'm sorry.

Mam   Where the hell do you think you're going?

Stuart   It's not what it seems.

Mam   She's only fourteen, Stuart.

Stuart   Honestly, I thought I loved her. I didn't know what I was doing.

Mam   You knew exactly what you were doing.

Stuart   Look at me. Look at me. I'm covered in fucking marmalade and you're having a go at me. Fuck this. Fuck you and your weirdo daughter and your spakker for a husband. I never even liked you. I never even liked her. I'm the victim here.

Mam   Victim!

Stuart   I've had a sheltered upbringing.

Mam   I'll give you a sheltered upbringing, you fucking monster.

She slaps him across the face. **Stuart** *picks up the knife. He holds it up. There is a stand-off.* **Mam** *grabs the blade and holds it tight, blood runs down.* **Stuart** *lets go of the knife.*

Stuart *stops dead.*

Mam   Get in that cupboard.

Stuart   Which one?

Mam   Get in the fucking cupboard. NOW!

Stuart *sheepishly goes into the cupboard.* **Mam** *rushes to* **Jill**.

Jill (*from inside the bathroom*)   Virtually the final scene. Jill is in the bathroom.

Scene Twenty-Two

Mam *outside the bathroom.* **Jill** *inside.*

Mam   Jill. What did he do to you? What did he do? Come on, sweetheart, open the door.

Jill   Please go away, Mam.

Mam   Jilly, open the door.

Jill   Mam, you don't want to see me now.

Mam   Jill, it's all right. Just open the door.

Jill opens the door and comes out covered in blood. She is holding the knife and has cut her wrists.

Mam   Jesus Christ.

Jill   I'm sorry, Mam. I couldn't even cut it properly.

Lighting change.

Jill   And then I fainted.

Mam *brings Jill a bowl of water. As she says the speech she starts to wash herself, cleaning up all the stage blood.*

Jill   And somehow Mam managed to pick me up. And she carried me across the landing. And everything was becoming too much. And Stuart was shouting from in the cupboard and her head was spinning and I was too heavy and she hadn't eaten for several days. And there we were at the top of the staircase. And she fell. And down we tumbled and I landed on top of her and she was shouting too because she couldn't get up and when we woke I was in the bed next to hers and we were both in hospital.

But somewhere in that fall. Somewhere in the middle of the staircase, something was irrecovably changed. And when I woke up I couldn't remember why it was that I'd tried to commit suicide. And I knew it was all right. Even if Dad was a cripple. Even if I was fat. Just as long as we didn't see that bastard Stuart any more. And Mam said she'd find a way so I never had to. And I asked Mam what had kept her going. Through everything that had happened. And she said she didn't know. But she said there was one time when she first brought him home. There was this one day when she just couldn't cope any more and she got all these pills and a bottle of whisky and lined them all up in a row. And just before she was going to take them, she heard Dad moan from next door and she went in to see him. And she looked down at his face and on it was a smile. Just a brief smile. For a second. And then it was gone.

And maybe life isn't about the tragedies. Maybe that's just what's normal, hurt and heartache, and loneliness and despair. Maybe life's about those tiny moments that keep us going through all that darkness. The little things. Like a delicious supper, or a tiny moment of kindness, or a smile – just for a brief second. Maybe it's about not giving up, and maybe we all have to try. But I'll tell you one thing life's bloody weird, isn't it?

By now a table has been prepared. **Mam** *dishes out some stew.* **Jill** *joins her. They both eat it.*

Scene Twenty-Three

Jill   Scene Twenty-Three. The Unbearably Glib Epilogue.

Mam   It's funny how things work out.

Jill   It's funny how all your problems can just 'disappear'.

Mam   I think we're actually quite happy now. Just the three of us. Me, you and your dad.

Jill   I think so.

Mam   I'm glad you've got that cooking thing under control.

Jill   I'm glad you're eating properly.

Mam   It's amazing what a good bit of catharsis can do.

Jill   It's funny that you can get rid of all your problems at one fell swoop.

Mam   I couldn't agree more, sweetheart.

Jill   Any more 'stew'?

Mam   Don't mind if I do.

They look towards the audience breaking through the apple-pie image with vicious sneers. A fanfare plays.

Dad *as Elvis appears with a mike in a ridiculous costume.*

Dad   Ladies and gentlemen, boys and girls, countrymen, comrades, brothers in arms, time is fleeting fast and as we move deeper into the night, we have finally come to the end of our humble show this evening. And good people all, I ask of you as you wend your weary way home this evening to stop and think about what you have seen tonight. Consider the marvels you have witnessed on our tiny stage, but I ask each and everyone of you to realise that what you have seen in these four walls tonight is only art. Don't weep or despair at the tragedy and horror we have depicted here. Instead remember that all the world's a stage and all of you good people in it are merely players and this vast and shimmering world of ours is all love and all light. And there are no cripple Elvises, no sad mams or Burger Kings, no fat girls or cake-makers, there are only people, human beings who love and hope and fear, who spend all their days in search of a little truth, a little happiness, a fragile little moment that will raise us up. And tonight, as you leave with your loved ones, raise up your voices and rejoice that we are all one, all snuggled together under the vast umbrella of God in the eternal kingdom of Heaven, transformed and exalted, ever glorified, ever uplifted, ever venerated in his everlasting love.

My name is Elvis Presley and you've been a very special audience.

He then sings 'Glory, Glory Hallejulah'.

He disappears.

Sound effect of 'Elvis has left the building'.

Bollocks

Bollocks was originally performed as the Radio 4 play *Gristle* on 19 January 1997. The cast was as follows:

Peter	Derek Walmsley
Mary	Tracey Whitwell
Ian	Trevor Fox
Lisa	Sharon Percy
Mr Happy	Shaun Prendergast
Man	Dave Whitaker

Director Kate Rowland

The stage play *Bollocks* was first performed as a rehearsed reading at Live Theatre, Newcastle-upon-Tyne, on 5 March 1998. The cast was as follows:

Peter	Derek Walmsley
Mary	Philippa Wilson
Ian	Trevor Fox
Lisa	Sharon Percy
Mr Happy	Shaun Prendergast
Man	Dave Whitaker

Director Max Roberts

Scene One

Monologue

Peter   I think it's only when you can't do something that you notice how weird it is. You know, like sex. How sex is everywhere. Everywhere you look it's on display. Every magazine, on the TV, everywhere. And you start asking yourself, what is it, this 'sex'? How to keep your man happy? Are you getting enough? Ten ways for the perfect orgasm. What does all this really mean? Why does it only happen to other people? Why is it always just out of your grasp? And the truth of the matter is I don't think all this sex even exists. In real life people aren't shagging each other senseless. Who do you know who's shagging all the time? In real life people are coming home from work knackered and reading about it in friggin' magazines. Nobody's got the time. And everybody knows that it's a load of bollocks, but it still doesn't stop you wanting it.

I'm reading all this stuff. Thinking all this mixed-up crap. And I can't even toss myself off. No secret little wank just to get it out of my system. It's just churning in my mind. A fucked-up churning. All I see is a sea of cocks and cunts and arseholes all getting fucked, all cumming all over. And at first it was sexy – feeling turned on all the time, but then it gets horrible, all these apertures disconnected from bodies. Like I'm being suffocated by hairy minges, like all these fat pricks are poking me in the face. And I want to scream. I want to say stop. I thought sex was something beautiful, I thought it was something sacred, I thought it was something you could touch and taste and feel. I thought it was the weight of another body. I thought it was the special privacy. I thought it was another person breathing in your face.

Intro to 'Banks and Braes' sung by Kathleen Ferrier.

Scene Two

Open ground, Northern Ireland.

The sound of feet tentatively creeping through broken rubble. We hear footsteps and nervous breathing as if someone was in danger. There is an air of unpleasant suspense. Suddenly there is gunfire.

A man lets out a blood-curdling scream. It is absolutely shocking and horrific. It goes on and on. As the scream goes on the singing gradually gets louder. The sound of the screaming is unbearable, but the singing crossfades and the beautiful elegy is all that remains.

Scene Three

Peter's *house.*

Mary   What have you been doing?

Peter   Just sitting.

Mary   You should have had a walk. It's a lovely day.

Peter   I didn't feel like it.

Mary   It'll do you good.

Peter   What good will it do me?

Mary   It might cheer you up.

Peter   Look, I don't need cheering.

Mary   I popped into me mam's on my way home. She's given us the three hundred quid.

Peter   What?

Mary   Here.

Peter   What did you say to her?

Mary   I told her we'd pay her back. But she says it's a present.

Peter   What a fucking bitch.

Mary   What are you on about?

Peter   You took it?

Mary   Of course I bloody well took it.

Peter   After what I said?

Mary   Yes, after what you said.

Peter   For Christ's sake.

Mary   What else was I supposed to do? Where else are we going to get three hundred quid?

Peter   Give her it back.

Mary   What are you on about, Peter?

Peter   We don't need charity. I've told you. I'll get a job.

Mary   Look, Peter. Normal blokes can't get work never mind . . .

Peter   A fucking cripple.

Mary   It's just to tide us over.

Peter   You realise why she gave you that money.

Mary   Because she . . .

Peter (*interrupting*)   To get at me. Don't you see?

Mary   Don't be so bloody stupid.

Peter   You don't even care.

Mary   Of course I care.

Peter   You've got a funny fuckin' way of showing it.

Mary   You're being ridiculous.

Peter   Look, just fuck off with your three hundred quid.

Mary   We can't go on like this much longer.

Peter   What do you mean? I'm fucking stuck with this for the rest of my life.

Mary   Come on, pet.

Peter   Don't patronise me.

Mary   I'm not patronising you.

Peter   I don't need fucking pity.

Mary   What about me, Peter?

Peter   What about you?

Mary   I'm the one that needs some pity. Have you ever thought I might need a bit of support?

Peter   Ah, fuck off.

Mary   Peter.

Peter   You and your frigging mother. A right pair of fucking martyrs.

Mary   Stop it.

Peter   At least admit it.

Mary   I can't take much more of this.

Peter   Just say it, will you. Just say you hate me. Just say the last thing you want to do is to spend the rest of your life with some cunt with half his fucking dick blown off.

Mary   Peter. Not again.

Peter   Just fucking admit it.

Mary   You'd prefer it if I did hate you, wouldn't you? Cos it would be easier. You could feel really bloody sorry for yourself. But it isn't that simple, Peter.

Peter   It is that simple. Of course it's fucking simple.

Mary   Look, I know it isn't going to be easy but we have to try and get back to normal.

Peter   Normal.

Mary   I'm trying my best, Peter, but you have to give me a break. (*Pause. Then in extreme frustration.*) Sometimes I want to just go upstairs and fucking top myself.

Peter   Sometimes I wish you would.

Long silence.

Peter   I'm sorry, pet.

Mary   It's all right, lover.

Intro to 'Drink to Me Only with Thine Eyes'.

Scene Four

A bustling pub.

Lisa   Peter, have you and Mary ever thought about having kids?

Peter   Why do you ask?

Lisa   I just wondered.

Peter   Not really. Why?

Lisa   I always thought you'd make a good father. And you could spend a lot of time with it.

Peter   What's that supposed to mean?

Lisa   Nothing. I'm just saying.

Peter   What about you?

Lisa   I don't know, Ian seems a bit weird about it.

Peter   Weird?

Lisa   You know what he's like. He's worried about his independence and that. He says it's the wrong time. But I mean, when is the right time. It's weird to think we've both got to this age without any kids. I think it helps keep people together, doesn't it?

Peter   But you've been together for about four year.

Lisa   But we're still not married.

Peter   But it's the same thing.

Lisa   Not really. I mean, I love Ian and that. But you know, things are never what you dreamed of.

Peter   What do you mean, like?

Lisa   I just thought he'd take care of things more. Things are a real struggle. He's earning some money doing guvvies, but you know, it's not what I expected.

Peter   Well, things aren't exactly blossoming for me either.

Lisa   You're doing all right.

Peter   Come on. I'm a bloody cripple, I can't get a job or they'll stop me sick, and I'm not even thirty.

Lisa   Well, you'd never tell.

Peter   Never tell what?

Lisa   That you got shot. You look pretty good to me. Plus you've got your pension.

Peter (*dismissively*)   Fucking happy days.

Lisa   At least you're alive. What more do you want?

Peter   I don't know what I want. That's the whole point.

Lisa   Just give it time, Peter. How's Mary?

Peter   To tell you the truth things are a bit difficult at the moment.

Lisa   How do you mean?

Peter   We're under each other's feet a lot.

Lisa   It's funny how things work out, isn't it?

Peter   What do you mean?

Lisa   I mean. How come I ended up with Ian instead of someone else? Instead of you even.

Peter   You wouldn't want to get stuck with me.

Lisa   It might not have been so bad.

Peter   Right.

Lisa   What's the matter, I'm still attractive, aren't I? For my age.

Peter   Of course you are.

Lisa   It's just I think I'd feel settled with someone like you. I mean, you're pretty straightforward.

Peter   You might be surprised.

Lisa   No. I think you're all right.

Peter   Everybody has their faults.

Lisa   What do you think my faults are?

Peter   I don't know.

Lisa   Come on. You can tell me.

Peter   What you see from the outside doesn't really tell you much. You never really know what's going on underneath, do you?

Lisa   That's a bit deep.

Peter   Look, Lisa, there's noting wrong with you. I'm the one who's screwed up.

Lisa   You're not screwed up.

Peter   Lisa. I'm a fucking cripple, man.

Lisa   You're not a cripple. I think you're just a bit depressed.

'Down by the Sally Gardens'. First verse.

Scene Five

Peter's bedroom.

Mary   Look, I'm sorry.

Peter   What about?

Mary   About before.

Peter   It was my fault.

Mary   Come here.

She kisses him.

Don't be so uptight. You can touch me, you know.

Peter   I'm sorry. I'm a bit distracted.

Mary   I love you, Peter.

Peter   Don't.

Mary   What do you mean, don't?

Peter   Don't touch me there.

Mary   It's all right.

Peter   I don't like it.

Mary   It's all right. There's nothing to feel embarrassed
about.

Peter   There's nothing there.

Mary   Don't you feel anything?

Peter   I've told you.

Mary   I just want it to feel good for you.

Peter   Look, it doesn't feel of anything – it's just
disgusting.

Mary   You're being ridiculous. Why would it disgust you?

Peter   Because I've got no dick. Why the fuck do you think?

Mary   Come on, Peter.

Peter   What's the fucking point?

Mary   I don't care. I just want us to be close.

Peter   Give it a rest, for Christ's sake.

Long silence.

Mary   Why don't you ever touch me any more? Just because you're injured doesn't mean we have to stop being intimate.

Peter   I'm just . . . you know. I just don't feel like it.

Mary   Where does that leave me?

Peter   I'm sorry. I'll get over it.

Mary   You keep saying that.

Peter   It just takes time. It doesn't exactly make you feel very sexy having your block and tackle blown off.

Mary   Peter. I don't care what you look like. I need to be physical.

Peter   Well, how am I going to fuck you?

Mary   I don't want to be fucked. I just want to be intimate.

Peter   Jesus.

Mary   We have to talk about it.

Peter   How do you think it makes me feel?

Mary   You need to talk about it. You need to get it all out.

Peter   Look. I've had half me fucking dick blown off. End of story.

Mary   You can still do things.

Peter Shut up, will you?

Mary It's not about fucking. You could put your fingers in me. You can lick me.

Peter Jesus Christ, woman.

Mary It's been so long, Peter. I just want something back. I'm the one who's been mutilated. I'm only twenty-five, Peter. I feel sore. All over my body sore. Just for a bit of contact. It might not be something you can see, but it's still fucking real. It's still mutilation.

Long pause

Peter I'm sorry.

'Come Ye Not From Newcastle'. First verse.

Scene Six

Bustling pub.

Ian Lisa said she took you out for a pint the other night.

Peter Yeah.

Ian She said you didn't seem too happy.

Peter I was fine. I just had a bit of a row with Mary.

Ian The trouble with you is you spend too much time dwelling on things.

Peter I haven't been dwelling on things.

Ian It's the same as last time we went out. You spend too long contemplating your navel. You want to stop all this moping around.

Peter How many times do I have to tell you? I am not moping around. Look, what's wrong with the fact that I might think abut things?

Ian You should spend less time philosophising and more time getting your end away.

Peter For Christ's sake.

Ian I'm just saying there's nothing better than a good shag to take your mind off things.

Peter Give it a rest.

Ian I mean, Mary's a game girl. You should try out a few new things. I bet she'd be up for it.

Peter What would you know?

Ian You can just tell.

Peter Has she been saying anything?

Ian She hasn't said owt, you stupid bastard. But it's obvious that you're not exactly Casanova.

Peter What's obvious?

Ian You're hardly going to charm anyone with that attitude. Looka. If Mary's not up for it, get some on the side.

Peter Just shut it, Ian.

Ian What's the matter with you?

Peter How would you feel if you were in my position?

Ian You have to think of it as an opportunity. I mean, right, you had your stint in the army. And then you came out, admittedly you took a drop. But you're all right. You're a hero, man. There's plenty of people with a lot worse than a limp going about. Anyway, just because you're a cripple doesn't say you're fucked. I mean, some people think it's an advantage. Look at that bloke in the wheelchair, he solved the mystery of the universe by writing through a straw. You've got to snap out of it.

Music. 'Blow the Wind Southerly'.

Scene Seven

Monologue.

Peter   When you think about it. If there isn't a God how can you judge anything? How do you know if something is good or bad, if there's no divine justice? If some guy shoots me, well, why shouldn't he? If there isn't a God what's to stop him?

I ask myself over and over. What was I doing in Belfast? And I still can't tell you. And what's happened to the Paddy that fired the bullet? Is he dead? Did he have his balls blown off? Or is he still down the Falls Road shaggin' like a fuckin' rabbit? And if it's true that there isn't a God, I should wish him well. Because everything we do is just an accident. If there isn't some divine justice then it's all just chance. There's wars and then they stop. You hate people and get over it. Things happen and they change. And no one gives a shit. It just happens.

Music. 'Blow the Wind Southerly'.

Scene Eight

Ian*'s bedroom.*

Ian   Don't you fancy it?

Lisa   Now?

Ian   When else were you thinking of? What's the matter?

Lisa   There's nothing the matter. I just don't feel like it.

Ian   You never felt like it last night either. Or any night come to think of it.

Lisa   Well, what do you expect? You've been getting at iz all day.

Ian   Come off it.

Lisa   Come off it, what?

Ian   You've always got some pathetic excuse.

Lisa   Just let it lie, Ian. I'm just not in the mood.

Ian   I don't have to put up with this, you know.

Lisa   Well, maybe if you made me feel a little better about myself then it would be different.

Ian   What's that mean?

Lisa   You never touch me unless you want a screw. You never ask what I'm feeling. You never try and sort things out.

Ian   What's there to sort out?

Lisa   Jesus Christ. Our situation. Having a family. You know fine well.

Ian   Look, I'm doing me best.

Lisa   Why don't you just behave like a normal human being?

Ian   Would you rather be with someone else?

Lisa   I want to be with someone I can talk to.

Ian   I bet you'd rather be with Peter, wouldn't you? Mr Sensitive. Has he got a bigger knob or something?

Lisa   Shut up, Ian.

Ian   That's it, isn't it? You still fancy him, don't you? Your childhood sweetheart.

Lisa   I don't fancy anybody.

Ian   Is that right, though? Has he got a bigger dick than me?

Lisa   Please, Ian. I'm trying to talk to you. I've been thinking about our situation and everything.

Ian   What about the situation?

Lisa   Well, I was talking to Lynn Folger.

Ian   What about Lynn Folger?

Lisa   You know she's a dancer.

Ian   She's a stripper.

Lisa   Well, erotic dancing.

Ian   Stripping.

Lisa   She makes a hundred quid a night.

Ian   Bollocks. A hundred quid. That scrubber.

Lisa   I swear. She says I could get some work.

Ian   Who the hell's going to pay to see you?

Lisa   Just shut up. I'm serious. I'm asking you.

Ian   What?

Lisa   How you would feel.

Ian   Well, how do you think I'd feel? I can't even get me end up and you're parading your arse to every fucker in town.

Lisa   Well, how else am I going to make any money?

Ian   Jesus Christ, we're not that desperate.

Lisa   How else are we going to start a family.

Ian   Well, the first thing you've got to do is get pregnant.

Lisa   It would just be until we get ourselves on an even keel.

Ian   We're getting on an even keel.

Lisa   I'm only trying to help.

Ian   Help. By suggesting you bare your arse in public.

Lisa   You sound like me dad.

Ian   What do you expect? What if you're 'dancing' and your dad walks in?

Lisa   He never goes to the Ship.

Ian   You're fuckin' twisted. You won't have a shag because you're too busy worrying whether or not you should go strippin'.

Lisa   You're not even listening to me.

Ian   I'm not listening. Well, you're doing sweet FA for me, pet.

Lisa   Where you going?

Ian   To have a wank.

Piano intro to 'Come Ye Not From Newcastle'.

Scene Nine

Interview room.

Man   How old are you?

Peter   Twenty-nine.

Man   And you were in the forces.

Peter   Army.

Man   What happened?

Peter   I got hit by a sniper.

Man   Where?

Peter   In Belfast.

Man   No. Where?

Peter   In the groin.

Man   In the knackers.

Peter   In the groin area.

Man   Painful.

Peter   But I'm all right now.

Man   But they've pensioned you off.

Peter   I was in hospital a long time.

Man   That's hard lines.

Peter   I mean, I can get around and that.

Man   And you're after some work.

Peter   Yeah.

Man   Well, if you're fit enough to work, what's the matter with the army.

Peter   I'm not fit enough to fight.

Man   But you're fit enough to work.

Peter   Yes.

Man   What's the matter with you exactly?

Peter   I told you, I got hit in the groin.

Man   Do you have a limp?

Peter   It's hardly noticeable.

Man   But you do have one.

Peter   It's not my fault. Look, I'm telling you I'm fit enough to work.

Man   Look, don't expect any sympathy from me, mate. I just need someone who can do the job. What qualifications have you got?

Peter   Qualifications.

Man   O levels and that.

Peter   I never did O levels.

Man   Jesus Christ.

Peter   I've got some CSEs. Maths, English and Metalwork.

Man   That'll not do you much good.

Peter   Look, it was fifteen years ago. I learned a lot in the army.

Man   Look, mate. I'm not looking for marksmen, you know.

Peter   Well, what type of work is it?

Man   Normally we get students from the college.

Peter   Students.

Man   Are you reliable?

Peter   Of course I'm reliable, I was in the army.

Man   And you don't mind weekends.

Peter   What exactly is it you're looking for?

Man   The Metro Bunny.

Peter   You what?

Man   There's a special suit and that.

Peter   You're joking, aren't you?

Man   Didn't he tell you?

Peter   Christ.

Man   Look, you can get out now with that attitude.

Peter   No. Wait a minute. It's just. You know. I thought it was something different.

Man   You go round giving balloons to kids and stuff. There's Metro Bunny and Mr Happy. And I can tell for a start Mr Happy's out of the question.

Peter   It's just . . . I mean . . . I was a soldier.

Man   Take it or leave it. It's cash in hand.

Peter   I don't know.

Man   I'm supposed to be doing this as a favour.

Peter   But people'll see.

Man   Who'll see, you're in a friggin' suit, man. Those students are lining up for this job.

Peter   And you're sure nobody will know?

Man   Look, mate. Take it or leave it. I'm sticking my neck right out for you. And the last thing I want is someone taking the piss.

Peter   All right.

Man   Two fifty an hour.

Door opens. Someone comes in.

Man   Start tomorrow. Here's Mr Happy.

Peter   Hello there.

Mr Happy (*in a joyous mood*)   Hi!

Short piano intro to 'I Have A Bonnet Trimed With Blue'.

Scene Ten

'Hark the Echoing Air'. A verse about Cupid.

Scene Eleven

The park.

Lisa   The problem is, Mary. I don't know where it's going any more.

Mary   What do you mean, where it's going?

Lisa   It's like I can't even touch him any more. I just feel disgusted by the whole thing. Not with him, more with me. I don't know, I just feel trapped.

Mary   But you just moved in together.

Lisa   I know. It's just made matters worse.

Mary   What does he think?

Lisa   I don't know. He never really talks. I mean, he's out most of the time. Whenever I see him all he wants to do is sleep, eat or have sex. He never talks about things. You know what he's like.

Mary   You don't think he's got someone else, do you?

Lisa   I think he's depressed. I know you've got your problems and everything but I look at you and feel jealous.

Mary   Of me?

Lisa   Well, it's obvious you love each other.

Mary   Is it?

Lisa   Have you ever thought of having children?

Mary   We haven't really thought of it.

Lisa   But you do want kids, don't you?

Mary   I suppose so, but . . .

Lisa   The thing is he knows it's what I want more than anything else. He just goes on and on that we can't afford it.

Mary   Maybes he's right.

Lisa   But there's never a right time. I've started saving.

Mary   Where are you getting the money?

Lisa   Promise not to say anything.

Mary   OK.

Lisa   Well, you know Lynn Folger. She got me in doing some dancing.

Mary   Stripping.

Lisa   Mary.

Mary   Are you out of your mind?

Lisa   It's the only thing I can see is going to change things. If I get a bit money behind me, everything'll be a bit different.

Mary   What does he say?

Lisa   He doesn't know.

Mary   What do you mean, he doesn't know?

Lisa   He told me no way should I do it.

Mary   He told you not to and you still did it.

Lisa   How else am I going to earn that kind of money?

Mary   How much do you get?

Lisa   Fifty quid a night.

Mary   Only fifty quid.

Lisa   It's only ten minutes' work.

Mary   But isn't it weird? Taking your clothes off?

Lisa   It's a bit weird.

Mary   Don't you feel dirty?

Lisa   I don't see what's wrong with it. I've got a nice body.

Mary   But still.

Lisa   What is weird is that they're so close. Like at the Ship in the Hole. It was packed. You could feel the heat, the pricks in their trousers.

Mary   That's awful.

Lisa   In a way I enjoyed it.

Mary   Weren't you embarrassed?

Lisa   I didn't really think about it.

Mary   You must have done.

Lisa   I wasn't embarrassed. Look, Mary. It's awful. I have to tell somebody. You've got to promise not to say.

Mary   Are you all right, pet?

Lisa   It wasn't the stripping. I knew about that. It was after I'd been on.

Mary   What's the matter?

Lisa   Something happened.

Mary   What happened?

Lisa   Well, the manager locked the doors. And somehow he gave one of the other lasses some money.

Mary   Some money.

Lisa   You know, some extra. She was really pissed by then.

Mary   Calm down.

Lisa   It was for 'a bit extra'.

Mary   What do you mean a bit extra?

Lisa   She went on with hardly anything on to start with. I mean, she wasn't really stripping. I could see from the back. We got changed in the loos off the bar. She sort of ran on and took her clothes off. Then she was going up to people. These blokes and fondling them and that. She was taking their pricks out their trousers.

Mary   In the pub?

Lisa   It was late. And she was putting them in her mouth. These dirty blokes. They were shouting. I was watching from the back. And then she took one of the blokes on to the

little stage and she put him in her mouth. Then he turned
her round and he was fucking her. She was on this table and
he was fucking her. And they came out of their chairs and
they were queuing up. Queuing up to fuck the girl and she
was just laughing. And they were going wild. And the young
lass I was with started crying. I felt sick. The place was hot,
my face was burning. I could feel myself wanting to be sick,
and I couldn't breathe. I told the young lass not to watch. I
went in the toilet and after a while the girl came through
with cum all over her. She was pissed off her head. And I
couldn't speak. I couldn't even speak to her.

Mary   And you're still doing it.

Lisa   I told them I was finished. But they said I didn't
have to go those nights if I didn't want to. That I could
just do a few dinner times, you know, when it's pretty
harmless.

Mary   Have you been back?

Lisa   A few times. It's good money, Mary.

Mary   But how do you feel?

Lisa   I feel awful.

Mary   Jesus Christ, Lisa. You can't do this to yourself.

Lisa   I know.

Music. 'I Have A Bonnet Trimmed With Blue'. A verse.

Scene Twelve

Monologue.

Peter   It's not just that it's humiliating that's depressing.
It's that it cuts you off. Being inside this big suit and
everything. It makes you see things. It's like the whole
Metro Centre is a dream. Shops and shops of endless things.
And you can tell most of the people they can't afford it.

Even when they've just spent a bloody fortune you can see in their eyes they can't *really* afford it. It's something I hadn't noticed before.

There's no proper light, there's no proper air. They've got a fake antique village with a fake river and a fake stone bridge made out of fibreglass. Where you can buy fake antiques, fake miners' lamps made in Hong Kong. And you're in this village where you can't see the sky. You can't see anything except all these stupid bastards who think it's a treat to be there. Nothing better to do. And I'm in a rabbit suit looking at them on the fibreglass bridge and I can hear the taped ducks quacking. And I try and imagine myself in a real village just to enjoy it. And I realise to these people the village *is* real. It's better than real because there's no duck shit, no rain, no problems. And I realise that these people think they're enjoying themselves. There's nothing better, except if they were drunk. And you might say what's wrong with it. It's only natural. But I realise there isn't anything natural in the whole bloody place.

And you know how you can tell. The kids. The kids are always miserable. That's why they need someone in a bunny suit. Because they're screaming and crying and you look in their mothers' eyes and there is real despair. Not just when you're having a hard day. This is real desperation. There they are on their own, with screaming kids, exhausted, surrounded by things they can't afford, and this is their life and there's no way out, and even if they didn't have the kids, and even if they did have the money, or a nanny – you know they know that this is all there is. The limit of their imagination. Somewhere they can't find their way out of, in the artificial light being approached by a six-foot rabbit.

Reprise of 'I Have A Bonnet Trimmed With Blue'.

Scene Thirteen

Peter's *house. The party.*

Ian All right. Which star would play you if they made a picture of your life?

Lisa That's stupid.

Ian It isn't. It's a question.

Mary Do you want another beer?

Ian Peter.

Peter I don't know. Who would play you?

Ian Bruce Willis.

Peter Bruce Willis. More like Danny DeVito.

Ian Divvint talk daft. That shortarse?

Peter Who do you think you are, like, 'Garth'?

Lisa What about you, Mary?

Mary I never watch films.

Peter Of course you do.

Mary On the telly. But I don't know who's in them.

Peter Julia Roberts.

Mary That skinny cow. She looks like she's ready for the morgue.

Lisa Well, who else?

Mary I don't know. Meryl Streep.

Ian For fuck's sake.

Mary What's the matter with Meryl Streep?

Ian You've got to be joking, haven't you? She's about as horny as a kick in the nuts.

Lisa   Does she have to be sexy, like?

Ian (*to* **Mary**)   Well, you're sexy.

Mary   Give over.

Ian   Don't you think so?

Peter   Of course she's sexy.

Ian   You're at your prime.

Lisa   What about me?

Ian   What about you? Just because Mary's sexy doesn't say you aren't. Peter always thought you were sexy. Didn't you?

Peter   No. I mean.

Lisa   You don't think I'm sexy?

Peter   I'm not saying that.

Ian   He's always had a hot spot for you if you ask me. Since you were at school.

Peter   Howway, man, Ian.

Ian   Come on, admit it.

Mary   Peter.

Peter   This is stupid.

Ian   What's stupid about it? Anyway. You never said yours.

Peter   What?

Ian   Film star.

Peter   There aren't any Geordie film stars.

Ian   Don't be a complete twat.

Peter   Harrison Ford.

Mary *laughs.*

Lisa   Harrison Ford.

Ian   Well, you know what they say about Harrison Ford. Don't you?

Lisa   What?

Ian   He's got a dick like a baby's arm.

Peter   What are you trying to say.

Ian   You see, these games are very revealing.

Lisa   Is it true, Mary?

Ian   She's blushing.

Lisa   It must be true.

Ian   Look, she's went beetroot.

Peter   Who would you be?

Lisa   Sharon Stone.

Ian   Look, she's still thinking about his dick.

Peter   Leave her alone.

Ian   Look.

Mary   I wasn't. Anyway.

Ian   Well, it's not how long it is it's what you do with it. Isn't that right, love?

Lisa   Why don't you see if you can shove yours up your arse?

Ian   I'll have to unwrap it from round me leg first.

Peter   Just leave it be.

Ian   What's the matter with you?

Peter   It's just getting a bit crude.

Ian   Fuckin' hell. You're a bit prudish these days.

Peter   Well, there's women.

Ian   That's sexism, that is. Mary, you're not embarrassed, are you?

Mary   Well . . .

Ian   See. Lisa?

Lisa   What's good for the goose is good for the gander.

Mary   You mean the other way round.

Lisa   What?

Mary   The goose is a woman.

Ian   What?

Mary   What's good for the gander is good for the goose.

Ian   You've lost me. Anyway, Peter, about your dick . . .

Peter   Shurrup, will you?

Mary   Peter.

Ian   There's no need to be like that.

Lisa   He was only joking.

Peter   I think it's worn a bit thin.

Ian   'Funaah-funaah.'

Peter   I just don't know why you have to turn everything into an innuendo.

Ian   I was only having a bit fun.

Peter   But you always take things too far.

Ian   You're embarrassed, aren't you? Anybody would think you're scared of sex or something.

Peter   I'm not scared of anything.

Ian   Maybe you feel inadequate.

Peter   What do you mean inadequate?

Ian   Cos you're a cripple or something.

Peter   I'm not the one who's inadequate. At least my lass hasn't got to go stripping.

Ian   What.

Silence.

What do you mean? Go stripping?

Lisa   Mary.

Mary   Peter.

Lisa   You promised.

Ian   I told you.

Lisa   It was only two or three times then I stopped.

Ian   You stupid bitch.

Mary   What did you have to say that for?

Ian   Am I the only one who doesn't know?

Lisa   It was for the money.

Ian   But I said.

Mary   Just let it lie.

Ian   Shut up, you.

Peter   Don't tell her to shut up like that.

Lisa   I can't believe you told him.

Ian   I expect you've paid three quid to see her snatch 'n'all.

Peter   Don't start getting funny, Ian.

Lisa   I did it for the money. You lot. All of you. All you do is sit round and moan. At least I went and did something.

Ian   What you going to spend it on, like? A new sequinned G-string?

Lisa   I've put it away. You stupid bastard.

Ian   For a rainy day.

Lisa   For a kid.

Ian   Well, thanks for telling me, like.

Lisa   I don't have to ask you.

Ian   Don't you think it might be helpful to include me in this if you want to get pregnant.

Lisa   I don't have to include you any more.

Ian   Who the hell do you think you are, the Virgin bloody Mary?

Mary   Shut up -- both of yous.

Ian   You'll not be able to bare your arse down the Dog and Parrot when you're eight months pregnant.

Lisa   All I want is to have a kid. Is that too much to ask? All I want is to have someone to love without having to get their permission. Someone who's not so depressed they don't even talk to iz. I want a reason to get out of bed in the morning. It's only natural. I mean. All these excuses, Ian. What's the matter with you?

Silence.

Mary   Another beer, anybody?

Lisa   Fuck off, Mary.

Music. 'Go Not Happy Day'. First few lines.

Scene Fourteen

Monologue.

Peter   I have these dreams. Nightmares really. That people are fucking Mary. I'll be in the living room and then I'll go to bed. And there she is being fucked by somebody. Usually people I know. Like the binman or my old sergeant major. And they're giving it rice in the bed and I just stand there frozen. And they carry on as if I'm not there. Then suddenly they'll look up and laugh. Some bloke shaggin' my wife laughing at me. In my own bed. And I want to die. Not out of embarrassment. I want to die because of what Mary's gone through. The last thing she'd do is be unfaithful. I know it's me. There's something sick in my mind. Something in me that wants to be humiliated. That wants to humiliate other people. And it makes me sick. I think I must be sick. I think there's something sick in human nature.

Verse beginning 'He wears a blue bonnet' from 'The Keel Row'.

Scene Fifteen

Office, Metro Centre.

Man   You're late back again.

Peter   Sorry. I got held up.

Man   I'll give you held up. You're supposed to be the Metro Bunny. There's people queuing up to have this job.

Peter   Look, I was only five minutes late. I'll make it up.

Man   I don't have to take your lip, just cos yer a war hero.

Peter   I'm sorry. It'll not happen again.

Man   You bet it won't.

Peter   I'll get changed then.

Man   You better hop to it. Get it. Hop to it.

Piano out of 'The Keel Row'.

Scene Sixteen

The pub.

Mary   Look. I don't know what I'm doing here in the middle of the afternoon.

Ian   I thought you might want to talk about things.

Mary   What do you mean?

Ian   What do I mean. Peter.

Mary   What about Peter?

Ian   Well, he seems to be going off the deep end.

Mary   He's just depressed.

Ian   He seemed more than depressed to me.

Mary   It's fine, honestly.

Ian   Are you OK, Mary?

Mary   I'm fine. It's you and Lisa I'm worried about. Where is she?

Ian   She's gone to her brother's in Middlesbrough.

Mary   Oh.

Ian   Do you want another?

Mary   No, I'm fine.

Ian   Well, don't sound so depressed about it.

Mary   Thanks for the drink. I think I should be going.

Ian   Is there something you're not telling me?

Mary   No.

Ian   Mary.

Mary   Ian. I'm desperate. He's never satisfied. It's morning, noon and night. Picking at me. I know I should have more patience.

Ian All you need is a good fuck, the pair of yous.

Mary Jesus Christ.

Ian What are you Jesus Christing about? It's true.

Mary Ian. The accident.

Ian What?

Mary He can't do anything. He's not all there.

Ian No bloody wonder he's going round like one o'clock half struck.

Mary I should never have told you.

Ian The selfish bastard.

Mary What do you mean?

Ian So there's nothing there. Not even a little bit.

Mary Keep your voice down.

Ian Christ.

Mary Please don't say anything.

Ian As if I'm going to say anything. So you can't make love?

Mary It's not as if that's all you have to do.

Ian What do you mean?

Mary I can't stand it any more. He's switched off. It's deformed him.

Ian Come on, lover.

Mary I'm at the end of me rope.

Ian You just need someone to hold you, Mary.

Mary Ian. You must never tell anyone. It would kill him.

Ian Shh. The poor bastard. He doesn't deserve you.

Ian *kisses* **Mary**.

Mary   What are you doing? You can't kiss me here.

Ian   Nobody's looking.

Mary   Look. I don't think we should do this.

Ian   Mary. You need someone. You need me. You want to be fucked. I can see it, Mary.

Mary   I just want everything to stop hurting. Screwing you won't help me. It'd only make matters worse.

An apposite (second or third verse) of 'The Stuttering Lovers'.

Scene Seventeen

Ian*'s bedroom.*

Ian   Don't worry, she won't be back until tomorrow.

Mary   Jesus Christ, Ian.

Ian   I want you.

They kiss.

Mary   What about Lisa?

Ian   I don't want Lisa. I want you. I need you. I want to put my tongue inside you. I want to fuck you, Mary.

Mary   He mustn't find out.

Ian   Nobody will ever know, Mary. Nobody will ever know.

Next verse of 'The Stuttering Lovers'.

Scene Eighteen

Changing room, Metro Centre.

Mr Happy   You know your trouble, don't you? You're morbid. That's your trouble. I'm not saying I'm not sorry for you and I'm not saying you don't do a good job. But

you're the most miserable Metro Bunny we've had.
Anybody would think you'd be happy. You know, pleased
with the fact you were bringing pleasure into people's lives.

Peter   For Christ's sake, leave me alone.

Mr Happy   Cheer up, man.

Peter   Listen, you're getting right on my tit end.

Mr Happy   Just listen to Mr Happy. Whatever way you
look at it life's not that bad. It's just ways of seeing. The
trouble is, my friend, you just see the problems. One man
sees a glass half empty, the other sees the glass half full.
You're playing right into their hands by this self-pity. That's
exactly what they want you to do. Collective action, that's
the only way forward.

Peter   Look, you've lost me there, pal.

Mr Happy   You were wounded, right. So you've got
something to complain about. But what's the point of
keeping it to yourself? Have you ever discussed with me
how you feel?

Peter   I don't want to discuss my problems.

Mr Happy   What's the matter with you?

Peter   I got hit in Northern Ireland.

Mr Happy   Show me your wounds.

Peter   I can't.

Mr Happy   Show me your wounds. Look, until people
are prepared to come out and admit to each other they're
imperfect, as long as they are determined to keep themselves
to themselves and perpetuate the myth that somehow
there's such a thing as normality, things will never change.
Look. Do you see that? That's a colostomy bag. Now you
wouldn't have expected that, would you? But I'm not
ashamed to show you.

Peter   I don't see why that makes you any happier.

Mr Happy   At least I'm not hiding anything. I'm working for a better society where people can lose their inhibitions and just enjoy themselves.

Peter   But even if you turned the whole bloody world upside down – you can't make people happy.

Mr Happy   You can but try.

Peter   Listen, every morning you'd wake up and worry about something, however fine the weather is.

Mr Happy   There is nothing we can't provide for each other.

Peter   What if you're a cripple? What if you lose your legs in an accident?

Mr Happy   Then we'll get you a wheelchair.

Peter   Well, what if you have cancer or some incurable disease.

Mr Happy   Then we will give you somewhere to convalesce. And we will do research. Christ, it's all just a matter of resources. I'm not saying we'll not die. I'm just saying we can stop the misery of being alive.

Peter   But what if someone is insane?

Mr Happy   Well, give him somewhere to be. Care and consideration. Medication if it helps. But you can still treat them like a human being.

Peter   But what about people who are sick even if they seem fit and well?

Mr Happy   What do you mean?

Peter   What if somebody's lost their genitals?

Mr Happy   Jesus Christ. You don't give up.

Peter   But it must happen.

Mr Happy   Well, they'd be buggered. But the important thing is you have to care. You have to share our pain.

Peter   What do you know about it? How the hell can you know what I feel? No matter how bloody clever you are. No matter how dedicated. You can never know shag all. What do you know about the bleeding? About the shame? Or the embarrassment? Or operations? Or the arguments? Or the frustration? You can't understand a bloody thing. And if you don't understand I don't want your sympathy, or your highfalutin ideas. I'd much rather you shut your hole. I'd much rather you all just fucked right off.

Mr Happy   Look into people's eyes, Peter. Today when you walk through here. Look and see the damage. We're all cripples somewhere deep down.

Peter   You make me sick.

Mr Happy   What do you mean?

Peter   You sanctimonious little bastard. Just because you piss into a plastic bag you feel as if you can tell me what's right and wrong. If I didn't need this job I'd kick your fucking arse for you.

Mr Happy   That's it. Let your anger out, my man. It's the only way to heal. Why should you suffer alone?

Intro to 'Have You Seen Owt a Ma Bonnie Lad'.

Scene Nineteen

Peter's *house.*

Peter   Where have you been?

Mary   I just had a drink, with Lisa.

Peter   It's just you seem to be seeing a lot of Lisa lately.

Mary   Shouldn't I?

Peter   What's happened?

Mary   What do you mean what's happened?

Peter   You've been dressing up more lately.

Mary   I thought you liked me dressing up.

Peter   But you stopped.

Mary   Well, I've started again.

Peter   Who is it?

Mary   Who is what?

Peter   I'm not stupid. Who are you seeing?

Mary   I'm not seeing anybody.

Peter   Don't deny it.

Mary   I'm not denying anything.

Peter   You think I'm a fuckin' idiot. That I'm going to sit round here while you go round like some ten-bob whore.

Mary   You're being ridiculous.

Peter   Tell me who it is?

Mary   Honest, it isn't anybody.

Peter *grabs her.*

Peter   Tell me who it is or I'll knock it out of you.

Mary   Please, Peter. You've got it all wrong.

Peter *whacks her.*

Peter   Bitch.

Mary   Stop it.

Peter *whacks her again.*

Mary   Stop it, Peter. Please.

Peter *hits her again and again.* **Mary** *screams. She sobs quietly.* **Peter** *goes to sit down.*

Mary   Stop it. Stop it. There isn't anybody else.

Peter   What are you doing to me? What are you doing?

Mary   It's hard enough as it is.

Peter   Jesus. I'm sorry.

Mary   You have to control yourself.

Peter   I'm sorry.

Mary   I'm going to the bathroom.

Mary *goes to the bathroom and locks the door.*

Peter   Oh God, Mary. I'm sorry. I know there isn't anyone else. I'm sorry.

Reprise of 'Have You Seen Owt a Ma Bonnie Lad'.

Scene Twenty

In bed – fucking

Ian *straining.*

Mary   Harder.

Ian   Look at me. Look at me.

Ian *comes. Long pause.*

Mary   If you could wish for one thing in the whole world right now. What would it be?

Ian   I don't really know. What about you?

Mary   I don't want to say.

Ian   Go on, you can tell me.

Mary   I wish he was dead.

Ian   For fuck's sake, Mary.

Mary   Well, you asked.

First verse of 'Down by the Sally Gardens'.

Scene Twenty-One

Metro Centre.

Lisa   Peter.

Peter   What are you doing here?

Lisa   I came to see you.

Peter   How did you know where I worked?

Lisa   I asked a few people. I thought you said it was security.

Peter   It's undercover.

Lisa   Undercover.

Peter   Yeah. You know.

Lisa   What exactly do you do?

Peter   Look. Will you promise not to tell anyone?

Lisa   I suppose so.

Peter   I'm the Metro Bunny.

Lisa   What?

Peter   You mustn't tell Mary. Or Ian.

Lisa *laughs.*

Lisa   I'm sorry.

Peter   What's so funny about that?

Lisa   Well, you know, the Metro Bunny.

Peter   Jesus Christ. Don't tell Mary.

Lisa   I didn't mean to upset you.

Peter   I don't know why you came. Why you've been snooping around.

Lisa   Look, Peter. I know you're not happy.

Peter   How can you say that?

Lisa   What?

Peter   How can you know?

Lisa   I want to help you.

Peter   You can't help me.

Lisa   You could help me.

Peter   What do you mean?

Lisa   You mean an awful lot to me. All I want is some comfort. I've always had a soft spot for you.

Peter   Don't be ridiculous.

Lisa   I'm just tired. Of it. He's a monster, man. I need to be treated different from that. I know I'm worth more than that. I'm sensitive to things. You know. I think about things. You've always thought about things. It's what I like about you.

Peter   Lisa, pet. I think you've got the wrong idea.

Lisa   Please, Peter.

Peter   You're just being ridiculous.

Lisa   Will you just hold me? I just want someone to hold me.

Peter   Why me?

Lisa   I just want a man to hold me. That's all.

Peter   I can't.

Lisa   I thought.

Peter   Well, you thought wrong.

Lisa   But the way you look sometimes.

Peter   But that doesn't mean anything.

Lisa   I'm sorry.

Peter   You don't understand.

Lisa   I know that.

Peter   You can't possibly understand.

Lisa   You need help, Peter.

Peter   Listen, pet. I'm not myself.

Lisa   Peter.

Peter   You better leave me alone.

Lisa   I'm terrified. What are we becoming?

Peter   We'll look back on this in a few years and have a good laugh.

Lisa   Will we?

Peter   Have a good fuckin' laugh . . . It's funny where you end up, isn't it? Who you end up stuck with. I mean, none of us are bad people. But we certainly make a fucking mess of things, don't we? The thing is I can't even put into words properly what the problem is.

Lisa   I just want somebody close to me.

Peter   Please, don't touch me.

Lisa   I just want somebody close.

Long pause.

Peter   Lisa. I'm sorry. You have to leave me alone.

Lisa   But you said yourself things weren't good with Mary.

Peter   It's not Mary that's the problem.

Lisa   I don't understand. What is the problem?

Peter   I'm the problem.

Lisa   I don't understand.

Peter   I think an affair with me would be more trouble than it's worth.

Lisa   How do you mean?

Peter   The accident. Lisa.

Lisa   The accident.

Peter   I'm sorry, Lisa. I can't be close to anyone. Please don't tell anyone.

Lisa   What do you mean?

Peter   I'm sorry, Lisa. I have to go.

Reprise of 'Down by the Sally Gardens'.

Scene Twenty-Two

Monologue.

Peter   Sometimes I am just walking. Along a street. And I see a child. And maybe the child has only one leg. Or a broken arm. Or is blind in one eye. Or has had part of his head removed in some operation. And the child looks at me. And comes running in his callipers.

And then I see a woman. With one of her breasts removed. Or someone from a car crash. Or she's had a hysterectomy. Or a bone-marrow transplant. And she's running too. And there's a man with elephantiasis. And a guy with a wonky spine. And there's people with leukaemia and diabetes. People with open wounds and septic sores and bleeding gashes. And they are all running and they are all standing next to me singing. In their croaked voices, with their tracheotomies and their ruined lungs and we are all singing.

Standing upright – or as best we can. And I am surrounded by cripples and invalids, the corrupt, the flatulent, the weak and the dying. And we all rise and sing as one voice: 'It's a long way to Tipperary'. It's that song. And they are doing the best they can. And their hearts are right there. But I can never understand why it's me. I can never understand why it's that song.

Music: 'Kitty Will You Marry Me?'.

Scene Twenty-Three

The park.

Lisa   Mary. I think we should talk.

Mary   Talk.

Lisa   Mary. I know everything.

Mary   What do you mean you know everything? Who told you?

Lisa   Nobody's told me anything. Not directly. Who would, it's too painful. I worked it out.

Mary   I'm sorry.

Lisa   For Christ's sake, Mary. Don't apologise. You deserve much more than this. If there's anything I could do. I'd do anything to make it better.

Mary   What do you mean? I fuck your boyfriend and now you tell me that's OK.

Lisa   Fuck my boyfriend?

Mary   You said you'd worked it out.

Lisa   Jesus Christ.

Mary   What had you worked out?

Lisa   Peter. I know what happened to Peter.

Mary   He told you?

Lisa   You bitch.

Mary   I'm so sorry.

Lisa   How could you do that to Peter? How could you do that to me? You're a little whore, Mary.

Mary   I'm sorry. Honestly. I don't know what I've been thinking.

Lisa   I know exactly what you were thinking. You dirty slut.

Mary   It's been well over a year, Lisa. And he told me things weren't good between you.

Lisa   A year.

Mary   I'm sorry.

Lisa   I'd wait ten years. Twenty years. A lifetime for Peter. And to do it with Ian. You know what he's like with me.

Mary   I haven't been thinking.

Lisa   He's a bastard, Mary. Do you think he cares about you? Do you really think he cares for you any more than he cares for me. The bloke is a headcase. He's a sick bastard, Mary. And if that's what you want. You can have him.

Mary   Lisa.

Lisa   You can both go and fuck yourselves until you're blue in the face. It's your funeral.

Mary   But Lisa.

Lisa   You asked for it.

Mary   I didn't ask for any of this. I didn't ask for anything.

Speech by John Major.

Scene Twenty-Four

Metro Centre.

Peter   I've been thinking about what you said. About suffering alone. Sorry about what I said. About the colostomy bag and everything.

Mr Happy   It's all right. I've got nothing to be embarrassed about.

Peter   It's just that maybe I've been a bit depressed and that.

Mr Happy   I'm privileged that you're sharing this with me.

Peter   It's just I think I've been unfair to Mary. You know, everything she's done. Everything she's put up with. She's like a bloody saint and all I've done is pick at her and ignore her.

Mr Happy   Well, you have to tell her.

Peter   But what can I say? How can I make up for all the shit I've given her?

Mr Happy   You'll find the words. Just go. Go now and the words will come.

Peter   I can't go now. I've got to work.

Mr Happy   Give me that suit.

Peter   What are you doing?

Mr Happy   I'll cover for you.

Peter   But . . .

Mr Happy   Lend me your ears, Peter. Lend me your ears.

Scene Twenty-Five

Peter*'s bedroom.*

Ian   Come on then. Get your kit off.

Mary   Ian, I brought you up here to talk.

Ian   We can talk any time.

Mary   Please, Ian. Listen. Lisa knows.

Ian   I don't care, Mary.

Mary   How can you say that? I didn't want this to happen.

Ian   Just forget it. She doesn't mean anything to me.

Mary   How can you say that?

Ian   Because it's true.

Mary   Oh God, Ian. Can't you just try to be more understanding?

Ian   Understanding. Is that what you want from me?

Mary   What do you think I want?

Ian   To be fucked.

Mary   Christ. What are you doing here, Ian? He's your best mate.

Ian   He's your husband. Come on. I need you, Mary.

Mary   Stop it, Ian. It's disgusting.

Ian   I'll tell you what's disgusting. A young woman crippling herself over something that didn't even happen to her.

Mary   Of course it happened to me. It happened to all of us.

Ian   Look, it wasn't your fault. What good is fucking yourself over when you could be fucking me?

Mary This is serious, Ian. I'm pregnant.

Ian You're what?

Mary It's true.

Ian Are you sure?

Mary Of course I'm sure.

Ian Have you seen a doctor.

Mary I've took enough tests.

Ian You'll have to get rid of it.

Mary Hang on a minute.

Ian You can't keep it.

Mary It's not that simple.

Ian Of course it is.

Mary It's not that likely I'm going to get pregnant again very easily.

Ian But he'll kill you.

Mary But he always wanted a child.

Ian But not like this.

Mary But what about me? Why should I be barren?

Ian Mary.

Mary Maybe I should leave him.

Ian What, when you're pregnant?

Mary It's your child too.

Ian Now hang on a minute.

Mary But you said.

Ian I never said I was going to get you up the stick.

Mary You bastard.

Ian   Look. I thought this was different. I thought we needed each other. That we were stuck in relationships that were suffocating us. I thought it was all clear. That for once in our lives we were being honest with each other. And now you spring this on me.

Mary   Listen, you were the one who sprung this on me. I thought we were being careful.

Ian   What more do you want me to do?

Mary   You don't understand anything, do you?

Ian   What do you want me to do? What did you expect me to say? Eh?

Mary   I don't know, Ian. I don't know.

Ian   Do you really want to go and live in some shit heap with me and raise a bairn? Is that really what you had in mind?

Mary   Ian. I never had anything in mind. That's the trouble. I was always getting through and I was always waiting for life to happen. I always thought it was just around the corner; one day it'd be different. And I'd imagine it in the distance and I'd put out my hands to touch it. It was such soft wonderful silk. And then I'd see my hands and they were rough and dirty and I pulled back in horror. Not at life. But at my own hands. I don't know if I can go on like this. Maybe I have to grasp things warts and all.

Ian   Jesus Christ.

Mary   I think we should tell him.

Ian   You can't. It'd kill him.

Mary   But he has the right to know.

Ian   Just think about this a minute.

Mary   All I do is think about it.

Ian   He'll crucify you.

Mary   Maybe I deserve it.

Ian   You can't do this. What about me? What will he do to me?

Mary   Is that all you care about, Ian? I always thought you were just some insensitive pig. You know, always the ladies' man. Always the one with the joke. But I've seen more than that. I know there's more to you. I see there is something special in you and I need you to help me. I need some support.

Ian   What are you trying to do to me? You don't know anything about me. This was all meant to be a bit of fun and all you do is whine. What do you expect me to do? You're not going to trap me. You can go back to cockless bastard.

Mary   Oh my God.

Silence.

Mary   I thought you loved me.

Ian   I never even liked you.

Sound of **Peter** *coming in downstairs.*

Peter (*off*)   Mary.

Ian   Shit.

Peter   Mary.

Ian   What are we going to do?

Mary   Shh.

Sound of **Peter** *coming up the stairs.*

Peter (*off*)   Mary.

Mary   Peter.

Peter   What the . . . What's he doing here?

Mary   I'm sorry, Peter.

Peter   What are you doing in my bedroom?

Ian   It's not what you think.

Peter   I can't believe this is happening. After what you said.

Mary   I was going to tell you.

Peter   How long?

Ian   About three months.

Peter   But you promised.

Mary   I didn't know how to tell you.

Peter   Get out.

Mary   Please listen.

Peter   Out.

Mary   Peter. I think we should go downstairs and talk about this rationally.

Peter   There's nothing rational to talk about.

Mary   Please.

Peter   You cow.

Slap. **Mary** *starts to cry.*

Ian   Get off her.

Peter   Don't dare touch me. If I start I'll kill you.

Ian   Peter, she's pregnant.

Peter   What did you say?

Ian   Look, you've got no right to take it out on her. You're ever so pleased with yourself, aren't you? Because you're a fuckin' cripple. But look what you've done.

Peter   You're monsters.

Ian   You're the monster. Look what you've done to her, man.

Peter   I don't understand. Do you love him?

Mary   Don't be stupid.

Ian   She doesn't give a shit about me.

Peter   What the fuck is she doing in bed with you, then?

Ian   She needs some warmth, Peter.

Peter   What do you know?

Ian   Are you blind?

Peter   But how could you do this? How could you humiliate her?

Ian   You don't humiliate a woman by screwing her, but you do by ignoring her. You don't even deserve her.

Mary   Get out. Get out, you bastard.

Scene Twenty-Six

Peter's *living room.*

Mary   I'm sorry.

Peter   I bet you had a good laugh, didn't you?

Mary   Peter.

Peter   I bet he laughed his balls off. I bet he laughed his knob off when he heard.

Mary   Nobody laughed.

Peter   You did. You just can't admit it. You used to laugh. I remember when we were married. Do you remember at the reception and we laughed till we both cried.

Mary   Peter. Stop it.

Peter   And you cried when I went to Ireland. You kissed me and cried. But when I left this house you were laughing. You were laughing because we had such great hopes. But you know something, Mary. When they brought me back, when I was in the hospital. You didn't cry once. You didn't laugh. You didn't cry. Not when I was there.

Mary You have no idea how much I cried.

Peter Mary. There used to be a time when you were jealous. When you used to worry about other women. Now that's something to laugh about now, eh. Remember how you used to be jealous. Eh?

Mary Yes.

Peter Well, no need for that now. No need to worry that I'm going to go screwing around. To me that's something to laugh about.

Mary Shut up.

Peter Laugh when you see some poor down-and-out bastard. Laugh when you see somebody worse off than yourself. Shall I show you? Shall I show you something to laugh at.

Takes off his pants.

There, there's something to laugh at. Look at the state of that. No, look, Mary. Face facts. Look at me. What can you see? They're not genitals. It's a joke. It's just burned-up, mutilated flesh. It's a joke. A sick ruddy joke. Go on. Have a good honest laugh.

Mary Cover yourself up.

Peter What's the matter?

Mary Peter.

Peter You don't seem to be finding it funny.

Mary You're scaring me.

Peter How could you be scared of me when I haven't even got any balls?

Mary Stop it.

Peter   What do you see, Mary? Be honest, tell me what you see.

Mary   Nothing.

Peter   Mary, for Christ's sakes, look at me. Just tell me what's left?

Mary   A body that's scarred.

Peter   Tell me what it's like, Mary.

Mary   It's just scar tissue. Where your cock should be is just rubbery skin, it's contorted and smooth, it's pink and red . . . Peter, it's not an ugly body, it's beautiful. But when I look at you now, I don't even see it, all I see when I look is your eyes. The same eyes when we first met. You always had sad eyes. But when you used to look it felt like I had strong arms around me. Like you would never let go. All I ever wanted was someone to protect me and never let go. And you were so strong, Peter, you were so tough . . . Now I look and all I feel is alone.

Peter   Are you scared?

Mary   I don't know. I still love you.

Peter   It's just you've got a funny way of showing it.

Mary   Peter. I'm sorry. I'll never forgive myself.

Peter   Look. I don't blame you for going with Ian. I think you're quite entitled.

Mary   I'm not asking for you to understand. All I want is for you to say you love me.

Peter   Look. You can go ahead. I'm going to move out. You can keep the lot. The house. The furniture.

Mary   No. Peter. It's you I want. You just have to forgive me. I didn't know what I was doing.

Peter   Of course you knew what you were doing. Why are you lying to me now? Maybe my fucked-up body makes you sick. But believe me, you make me sick. Your slimy hands, your sagging tits, your fat arse, your stinking gob. Everything about you. You repulse me. You're rotten to the core.

Mary   Why don't you just hit me again? That's what you want, isn't it? Go on.

Peter   You're not worth the effort.

Silence. Over a long time. **Mary** *starts to cry.*

I used to think you were so strong compared to me. But you're just as broken as I am.

Mary   I don't want to leave you.

Peter   You're just a poor pathetic cunt like me, Mary. Look, I'll leave you alone.

Mary   I'm not leaving you now.

Peter   I think we should just go our separate ways.

Mary   Peter. Be reasonable.

Peter   There's something in us deeper than reason. I just need to be alone.

Mary   Are you serious?

Peter   Of course I am.

Mary   But what am I going to do?

Peter   At least you're strong and healthy. But if you're tied to me, pet, you haven't got a snowball's chance in hell.

Mary   Where are you going? Don't leave me alone.

Peter   I haven't the strength to look after you. I haven't the imagination. I'd been blind to all this before. It's got nothing to do with you and Ian. It's got nothing to do with us. It's just me. I can see too clearly.

Mary   For Christ's sake, don't do anything stupid. Not after what we've been through. Look everything's going to be all right again. Just the two of us.

Peter   Look, Mary. I don't want to see you again.

Mary   But we can make it work, Peter. No matter what you put me through, I'll still love you. I'll do anything to make things better. Just tell me you love me. Just say you still love me and it will all be all right.

Silence from **Peter**.

Mary   Just tell me, Peter.

Silence.

All you have to say is you love me.

Long silence.

Scene Twenty-Seven

Monologue.

Peter   I remember when I was small. The canary my granny had. I'd been out running around. Soldiers – some daft shite. And as I came in running I saw her standing with this pin. And the little thing was flapping at the bottom of its cage. And its eyes were just bloody lumps. And she was shaking like she didn't know what she'd done. And I grabbed her. I was shouting. And she kept saying it's what her mother did. It makes them sing better. And I was standing and I couldn't believe it. How she could be so cruel? And I was shaking too and I didn't know what to do. So I hit her, in the face. And I ran upstairs. I could hear her crying. And I was crying too, not for punching her. But because I understood. Something about why she had done it and to this day I've tried to put it into words. But it seems so hard. But it was something about how the world seemed clearer in the dark.

Final verse of 'Down by the Sally Gardens'.